Waking To Tears

Waking To Tears

Losing a Loved One to Violence

Compiled by
Traci Bieber Nelson

Writers Club Press
San Jose New York Lincoln Shanghai

Waking To Tears
Losing a Loved One to Violence

Writers Club Press
an imprint of iUniverse.com, Inc.

For information address:
iUniverse.com, Inc.
5220 S 16th, Ste. 200
Lincoln, NE 68512
www.iuniverse.com

ISBN: 0-595-17875-8

Printed in the United States of America

Waking To Tears is for everyone who's lost a loved one to violence. For every violent death there are too many of us who are left behind to carry a lifetime of pain. Share in our tears.

EPIGRAPH

No one can imagine the pain endured, no one can feel the instant loss of a loved one, no one can feel the anger, sadness and emotional roller coaster of violence unless you have lived to lose a loved one to the senseless act of violence.

CONTENTS

Epigraph vii

Preface xi

Acknowledgments xiii

Editorial Method xv

List of Contributors xvii

Introduction xix

Losing More Than A Son 1

Things I Miss About You 5

He was My Dad, I Never Said Good-By 7

My Only Daughter 9

Tears of Fear 10

A Vow 33

Please Carry Me 35

A Homicide Survivor? Who Me? 38

Memorial for Sean Alan Burgado 41

The Breath of Spring 44

3 Years Gone 46

You Should be Getting on with Your Life 53

Kevin 55

In Loving Memory 58

My Forever Friend 60

Carmen Amicae Meae Carissimae 63

Memories of a Home 65

Remembering Kyle 68

Reckless Horseplay is Murder: Joshua Eugene Hedglin 74

I Miss BET'O 84

Ripples in the Pond 86

The Howling 88
Our Angels 91
Gypsy's Angels 95
Abandoned Again 101
My Memories of Carl and Valda 108
Silence Kills 110
Not Even Death Will Keep us Apart 113
Gift of Love 115
My Mother and My Brother were Both Murdered 118
How I Feel 121
My Dear Sisters Murder 126
Epilogue 137
Conclusion 139
About the Author 141
Notes 143

PREFACE

On August 28, 1963, Martin Luther King Jr. made history with his "I Have a Dream" speech. On April 4, 1968 Martin Luther King, Jr. was shot to death, a victim of violence. John F. Kennedy was sworn in as the 35th President on January 20, 1961. On November 22, 1963 John F. Kennedy became a victim of violence. He was the youngest man to be elected as president and the youngest to die.

On September 21, 1947 my father was born. On March 2, 1980 he became a victim of violence. On June 6, 1947, my mother was born. On April 18, 2000 she became a victim of violence.

I can't begin to compare my parents' existence to the history made by Martin Luther King, Jr. and John F. Kennedy but they all have something in common, death by violence.

Martin Luther King Jr. had a dream and I have a dream too.

I have a dream of having parents.

I have a dream of my daughters having grandparents.

I have a dream for no one to feel the pain that I have lived with of losing not one but both my parents to violence. The painful heart, with a void that was once filled by my parents. A void that stays with you for the rest of your life, the pain doesn't go away but we have to learn to accept part of the pain.

We live in a disposable fast paced society. Finding the quick and easiest way through life. Does this mean we take others lives when we are not happy? Does this mean we rob, injure and kill someone because we don't like his or her beliefs, race, religion, sexuality, opinions or decisions? Does this mean when we are not happy with ourselves we take our own life or kill others?

There is no clear answer to violence but changes must be made. Violence can strike no matter where you live, no matter what race, religion, occupation, or social status—violence knows no boundaries.

I do believe that with violence, our children, our future, must understand that when words are said out of anger, those words can be taken back. When a person commits a violent act that act can NOT be taken back. A split second can change many lives and kill. We must learn to find other solutions to violence.

ACKNOWLEDGMENTS

When tragedy strikes a family there are many people around for the first month. Too often it seems after the funeral many of us are left standing alone. We don't know whom we can talk to or if anyone will understand the pain that is carried with us each day. I give thanks to everyone who believed in me while working on this book.

Thank you to all the organizations that helped in the collection of submissions for this book. Thank you to all the families who have communicated with me over the past several months, we have shared a pain that only we can understand. I have learned I am not alone in the quest for peace in my heart.

Thank you to my Higher Power for belief, hope, strength and the courage to face each day. Thank you to Pastor Douglas, Pastor Laurie, Priscilla and Aunt Nancy who helped guide me on my spiritual path.

For over twenty years the following people have offered love, care, belief and helped pick me up when I was falling: Aunt Grace, Aunt Mary, Kathy, Nana and Roni.

Thank you to Craig, Danielle, Lana, Sondra, Tracey C. and Tracy R. for always lending a shoulder to cry on and an ear to listen.

I have deep respect and appreciation for friends who have been there at a time I needed someone the most and give thanks to them: Bernadette for her unconditional support and Mary for reminding me that it's okay to be me.

A person can enter our life for a reason, season or lifetime and we don't always know who or how long that might be. Neal has helped me heal, shown me that I am still alive and can feel. Thank you for your patience, faith and giving me a chance.

Words could never explain the sisterhood friendship between Paula and I. We have shared many experiences and she could never be repaid for her love, concern and care. She's a friend that you can call at all hours of the day and listens without judgment. I thank Paula for believing in me and for being a true friend.

I could never give enough thanks to Wally. He's a patient and caring person in a world that can feel lonely and cold. His perspective of life is a gift that is generously shared with those around him. Thank you for believing in me, you are a safe friend.

One person in this world who knows me better than anyone else is my Mem. She has always been my safe haven. Mem never stopped believing in me and taught me valuable life lessons. When I feel like my life has too large of a void, I think of her words reminding me that my life didn't get here overnight and I won't accomplish everything in a day. Thank you for loving me unconditionally. I love you Mem and don't sweat the small stuff.

The three most important people in my life are my daughters. *I love you*. They are my light and love. I could never give enough thanks to my Higher Power for my three little blessings. When life is rough I remind myself of all that I am thankful for in my life, especially for my daughters' love, life and health.

Thank you Mom and Dad for bringing me into this world. I learned what love is and isn't. I learned what is precious in life can be taken away from us in a moment. I miss both of you. I miss what will never be. You will always be a part of my life as I am a part of you. *I love you*.

EDITORIAL METHOD

The letters, poems, essays and speeches shared have not been edited. The writings are their emotions, thoughts and lives expressed through their own words.

Each story includes the month and year of the loss. Stories are listed in alphabetical state order. Some chose to dedicate their writing by using a full name, nickname or preferred not to use their name. No matter how they signed their writing, they have shared a valuable part of themselves with everyone.

List of Contributors

Over several months I corresponded with people from all over the world. We have different experiences but a similar pain of losing a loved one to violence. This book wouldn't be possible without their help. Everyone opened their hearts and was willing to share their pain and loss. I applaud them for their courage to voice their perspective of their own lives. Thank you to everyone who has shared his or her life with me and to remind us that we are not alone.

INTRODUCTION

Someone once told me that I am a member of an exclusive club. The only way to be a member of this club is for someone you love to have their life ended by violence. Once you become a member you are a member for life. Welcome to the inside of our exclusive group.

Until I met other members, as I will call them for the moment, I felt alone. I felt no one could ever understand my feelings. At times I was told to *get over it, move on with my life* and even told I was *crazy*. Is it so *crazy* to have feelings of loss, resentment, grief, anger and unanswered questions? No, it's called reality and the reality is we've had a loved one murdered. There I said it. Murder the dirty little word that has changed our lives.

I have learned over the years there are safe people you can talk to and then there are people. The safe people are the ones you can tell exactly how you feel and not be judged. There aren't many safe people in this world. When you experience trauma, you learn who the safe people are in your life.

Even though it took me years to find safe people, they are the people that have helped me deal with reality. My reality of witnessing the shooting death of my father in 1980. The reality of my mother bludgeoned to death by my stepfather who then shot himself to death in 2000. The reality that the people who brought me into this world are gone.

I honestly didn't think I could deal with all the pain. For twenty years I had stuffed away the pain of losing my father. I adored my father. I could never accept his death and finally started to in 1999. I thought I was making some progress when I got THE call. The kind of call that wakes you in the wee hours of the morning, waking you to tears. This call brought the news of my mother's death. I couldn't believe the woman I admired; the woman I loved and missed was now gone.

The mission of this book is two-fold. First, I hope someone in this world will not feel as alone. They will find some sort of small comfort in knowing that there are too many of us who live our lives with a void that will always be a part of us. Our grief and experiences may differ but our grief is not an isolated emotion. Second, I hope society will see that for every violent death there are too many of us left behind to cry, grieve and flooded with emotions. We are forever changed. Think about us the next time that you hear of a shooting, domestic violence, robbery, a MURDER.

LOSING MORE THAN A SON

October 1991

My eighteen-year-old son, Brian, was robbed and shot to death nine years ago this month, by three gang members in our nice, quiet neighborhood of country mailboxes and horse properties. Brian died a brief time later, never regaining consciousness, nor did my husband and I and his then fourteen-year-old sister have a chance to hold him, comfort him or kiss him one last time before death claimed him.

Instead a police officer came to our door to unleash the horror that began the nightmare for us. We, my family and I, have survived the murder of our son, but it has been a most difficult journey and we are forever changed by this traumatic and devastating loss.

We lost our only son. My husband lost the only male left in our family to carry on the family name. My daughter lost her dear brother and only sibling then. Our four-year-old daughter lost the big brother she will only know as a murder victim. I lost a piece of my heart and soul that I will never get back. We lost the grandchildren Brian would have given us. His sister's children lost the uncle they will only know as a murder victim. Countless other family members and friends lost Brian. We all lost so much as a result of this act of violence for a few dollars in his wallet; our trust that the system worked as his killer only served seven years for the murder and our belief that if you lead a good life and try to be honest and raise your children well that this type of horror will not touch you.

Murder can touch anyone at any time in this country. That is a fact that is not easy to live with, but if more would accept it and fight for the changes that could ensure a safer, healthier world for our future we would all be better for it. We must all become involved even in simple ways of voting responsibly and mentoring troubled youth, or reaching out to those in need within our own circle of family and friends.

Whatever happens in my life though, despite my survival, all the happy events of subsequent births and weddings, graduations and holidays, are always over-shadowed by the death of my son and the knowledge of what he does not share with us but should. It is akin to every sunny day being mixed with storm clouds. You never just get to enjoy the beauty of the blue sky without the anger of the dark storms. I am always and will always be the parent of a murdered child. I cannot change it and I cannot run from it. I have learned to live with it and the endless pain of his loss, but it was a choice and it is a choice I have to commit to over and over again when the pain brings me down, such as this month, October, both his birth month and his death month.

On Brian's birthdays, I light a candle saying "Happy Birthday, dearest son." On holidays I do the same. On the anniversary date of his murder, I light a candle saying these words, "Happy Heaven Honey." It is the only thing that works for this day of sheer emotional hell and yet the tears fall, and my heart is heavy and my soul cries for my son who in my minds eye is "forever eighteen" though he would be twenty-seven this month. I know he is in a better place but damn it I miss him so and want him here with me.

I love you dearest Brian. I always will.

Dearest Brian:

It has now been over nine years since you were torn from our lives by the senseless greed of another, your same age. I resent the passage of time, as it mocks my grief with daring to move forward. I have survived and gone on to give meaning to the pain that endures forever, and yet, my heart is always half-mast without you.

I resent the emotional energy that I had to expend in attempting to get the one who shot you to death for your wallet in prison for murder. He only served seven years for aggravated robbery, due to a plea agreement give him wrongfully. I want to forget him. It is hard enough living without you. There is so little energy left for him. Yet I must. If I do not try, a cold-blooded murderer will walk the streets again, as you did that fateful morning-in his path and the path of two bullets marked for you. (And now he does).

This year you would have been twenty-seven-years-old. You would undoubtedly be married with children of your own. You were so good with kids. My last memory of you, the day before you were killed, is of you cradling two-month-old Tracey in your arms, cooing to her attempting to coax a smile from her colic fussiness, while I tended to others in my home day care. I thank God for that special moment. We could have been arguing about your quitting some of you college classes. We could have been arguing about the usual things a mom and so argue about when she realizes her son is growing away from her into his own. I am so grateful the last few minutes I was allowed to share with you were tender.

It is hard to see your friends, grown and married, having children. My heart is happy for their gain but crying for what I will never share with you–what we were robbed of too.

Your sister has had such a hard time dealing with the pain, the anger and the fear. A fourteen-year-old, when you were killed, not capable of accepting the horror of learning of her own mortality-through yours-and that another can take a life so easily, so cruelly. Missing her brother, her only sibling then, learning life does indeed go on and wondering, as I do, how it can. I know you walk each step of her journey alongside her, as with us. I am comforted by that fact, and still we miss you more than words can ever truly express.

Your father lost not only you, an extension of himself, but the last bearer of his family name. You were the only male to carry on the tradition of countless generations. Gone-lost forever. His grief is different than mine-intermingled with rage, powerlessness. A father, a man, always wants to be his family's protector from all harm. He could not save you from another. It burns in him, the cruel unfairness of it all. If you could see his gentleness, his joy, with the new baby we adopted, the sister who will never know you, you would know he will be okay. His demons of grief will diminish with time. The anger will slowly burn away with the cleansing of healing tears and the fading of fresh, raw rage.

We owe it to ourselves and your memory to go on. To forge ahead and live and laugh again. It would have been so tempting, to allow the heavy burden of sorrowful grief drown us. It would have been easy to give in to the darkness-the void of living without joy. So much of our joy was taken that it amazes me there is any left. Your new sister showed us there was. She breathes so much happiness and life back into this family with a missing piece.

I never thought I could experience absolute joy again, once you were ripped from my heart. I did-and I realized you give me permission. I hear it whispered in the wind blowing through the branches of the tree planted in your memory-Brian's Tree. I hear it in the memories of who you were in life, warm, compassionate, and serious-knowing your life would end this way. I hear it in my heart and from above. I know it is right and honorable to take a mother's love, through grief, and wrap it-a precious gift-around another. You would have loved your new sister dearly, as your first sister.

Dearest son, who once gave me the meaning of life, now I give life the meaning of you in honoring your memory with truly living again, despite the endless pain. I thank God for the eighteen years we shared together. It should have been more and in many ways it is. Thank you dearest one.

Love always,
Your family

~Beckie A. Miller, Arizona

THINGS I MISS ABOUT YOU

January 1999

I miss your goodbye kisses as you went off to work each day and I miss your "honey I'm home!" as you came thru the door at the end of each day.

I miss your gentle snores that slowly became like "white noise" in the background so I learned to rely on them to sleep.

I miss the way you always smiled when we caught each others' eyes across a room and the way my heart always skipped a beat at that smile.

I miss the silent comfort of just sitting quietly with you.

I miss the way you came to bed and snuggled up on cool nights so I could warm you up and the way you whispered "I Love you my soft warm wife, my love of my life" and then kissed the back of my neck as you snuggled up and fell asleep.

I miss the way you danced with me in the kitchen when we both tried to do something and it got too crowded and we'd laugh and hug and dance.

I miss the way you always swore you married me for my spaghetti sauce.

I miss the way you looked at me and touched me gently when we made love.

I miss making Christmas cookies for you and hard-boiled eggs at Easter so you could have your deviled eggs.

I miss the way your face got all soft when special love songs came on.

I miss being your copilot and reading maps for you on our road trips.

I miss the way you played with our son and cried over the loss of our daughter.

I miss the way you learned to like the TV shows I liked and turned down the volume on the TV when you watched something I didn't like (or put your earphones on).

I miss fixing things around the house with you.

I miss "spooning" with you at night.

I miss the way you said "I love you wife" and I never doubted it was true.

I miss the safety of knowing I could make you mad at me and that you still loved me with all your heart.

I miss buying you t-shirts with silly sayings and cooking for you and rubbing your back.

I miss you my love…I miss you…to Bob from Deb with love.

~ Debbie Curry, Arizona

He was My Dad, I Never Said Good-By

April 1999

I don't know what to say. I'll just say what I feel. I do know how bad I feel and how much pain I feel inside. I know how bad I miss my Dad. How bad I want to see him, and hear him talk. It seems like yesterday since we lost him. The pain still feels very fresh and overwhelming. There are times when I don't know how I go on, living day to day. I know I miss him a lot and just want to see him, and hug him and talk to him. I can still see him smiling and hear him laughing. I remember the way he used to sit, with his arms on his knees, and the way he carried himself when he walked. He was my Dad, I never said good-by.

He raised me and cared for me and I always knew he was there for me. I no longer have that. I no longer have my Dad. I don't understand why. He had many years left to be with me. I don't understand why he was taken from me. I don't understand why someone would want to take another persons life. So, many lives have been ruined because of Mr. R's actions, because he thought it was OK to kill my Dad.

My Dad was a Father, a brother, a son, an uncle, a grandfather and a great grandfather. All these children no longer have a grandfather or great grandfather to call TaTa anymore. All these children have lost their innocence. Innocence lost to a violent crime, to murder of somebody so dear and close to him or her.

Violence, pain and loss are now a big part of all our lives. Not only did Mr. R put a knife through my Dad's heart; he put that knife through all of our hearts. We have to live with the pain he has caused. What gives him the right to cause so much pain to so many people? So many lives have been ruined. We have to face the pain on a daily basis. It's very difficult to face the world and go on; knowing your Dad was brutally stabbed to death.

I often wonder what was going through my Dad's mind the night of his death. He was all alone in the dark. Did he cry for help? Did he suffer? Did he think of us, his children? Did he think of my Mom? Was he able to pray?

With all the sleepless nights and endless days of thinking I feel like I have aged a great deal. He was my Dad, I never said good-by. I never thanked him for being my Dad. I never kissed him good-by. This pain I am going through, I hope and pray nobody has to go through. At times it seems unbearable. My Dad was big part of my life. Now there is a big void where he once was. Holidays and family get togethers are so very difficult, because of the emptiness that now comes with them. The emptiness of my Dad not being there anymore. The emptiness of knowing he was taken from us in such a brutal and horrifying way. Knowing that he would still be with us if Mr. R had not taken him away from us. My Dad had every right to live. Who is Mr. R to change that? To change and ruin so many lives forever.

He was my Dad, I never said good-by.

Rest in peace Dad...Natalie

~Natalie, Arizona

MY ONLY DAUGHTER

March 1998

When did I first love you?
Was it when you were due?
Was it when I first held you?
And now that you've gone to a better place,
I'm sure you ware his royal lace.
For now that you are gone there is no smile upon my face.
The man who took your life waits for his place.
There will be no peace until he is deceased.
The tragic death you suffered will always live with me.
I was not there to protect you from that beast.
My daughter you are always loved and missed.
I know you are in a better place.
For now I send you my love and kiss.
Love Mom

~Brenda Bratton, Arkansas

TEARS OF FEAR

September 1997

In May of 1985, I began dating the man I thought was going to be in my life forever. He was older than I was. I was 17 years old Wayne was 24 years old at the time. I had enlisted in the Armed Forces and was scheduled to leave for Basic Training that July. I had went through a bad break up with a previous boyfriend and was looking to date somebody that he didn't know, so he couldn't terrorize me the way he had been. I met Wayne through a mutual friend from high school. It was my senior year and I thought I had so much life ahead of me when I got home from Basic Training…Boy! Was I wrong?

I spent 6 months in Basic Training, but was put on medical hold at the end of my cycle, due to the fact that I had bad feet and I think maybe a bad attitude too. Wayne and I wrote to each other quite frequently while I was gone. One day, I called home to talk to him, which I had moved all of my things into his house right before I left, and he gave me an ultimatum. He told me I either came home or he was moving on to greener pastures. I should have stayed, but I didn't. My C.O. came in to visit me while I was in the hospital and told me that I pretty much had to leave because it was deemed I was going to need many years of foot surgery and after the first one, I wouldn't be able to perform my job. So, I accepted the Enlistment Level Separation he offered me. I was put on a recall list to go back after 2 years. Needless to say, three days after I was discharged from the Army, I got pregnant with my first child, a son.

Wayne never believed my son was his kid. I didn't even know I was pregnant until I was almost 5 months along. I was still having my periods. In that time, Wayne's whole persona changed towards me. What I once thought was a generous, fun-loving kind of guy, quickly turned into a controlling, eerie kind of guy. He began controlling my contact with my family and my friends I had since the beginning of high school. He moved me up to California where he rented a house and said we were the managers while we lived in this house. I soon found out that wasn't his whole idea of renting this particular place. It was in an isolated area in Northern California and the nearest neighbor was about a ¼ mile away. He told me he thought it would do me some good to go through a cool down period after 6 months of learning how to be an aggressive soldier.

I never knew I was pregnant with my son until I was almost 5 months along in my pregnancy. I had my periods and was only getting sick at midnight, so I thought nothing of it. I thought we were going to be so happy the 3 of us and live a happy, normal and healthy life. I was wrong about that too. Our first love spat, happened while we lived in Payne's Creek and it was a far cry for help. He began to slap me around and then he pushed me through a screen door. I started to cry and said I'd rather die than live like this with him. The next thing I knew, he grabbed his 22. Revolver and put a bullet in the chamber and spun it around. He then put it to my head and began to pull the trigger. When he got to the third time, I begged him to stop and said I wanted to live. I never told him I wanted to die again, but I did wish I could die many more times in our relationship.

As you can probably imagine, just as most people who have lived in a domestic violence situation, things did not get better over the years. I lived with Wayne for twelve and a half years. And after my son was born, I became pregnant with my daughter six years later while taking birth control pills. I never have and never will say that I regret having the two wonderful kids that I have now. They are still my number one priorities and I love them with all of my heart. I think they both know how much now.

Though I lived not knowing from one day to the next as to what kind of mood Wayne would be in or what was going to set him off next, I continued to push myself on. Just wishing that someday my prince would come and take me away from this horror and pain.

It would probably take me another book to even go into all of the details of the strange and twisted life I lived with this man whom I loved and gave birth to his children. For eight of the years that we were together, Wayne's mother lived with us and for a short period, up until her death, his grandmother too. I never understood why it was that Wayne would never tell me he loved me, until I started to see for myself, the relationship he had with his mother. He was raised without a father, but his older brother was more like his father figure growing up His brother had his own life though and had his own issues he had to deal with on a daily basis as well. From the time that I had been with Wayne, he never worked a "real" job. He dealt drugs for a majority of our life together, constantly telling me that it was all he really knew and also telling me that he had worked way too hard all of his life and he didn't think he should have to work hard now. He was always buying into the quickie "get rich" schemes that you would see in magazines and on television. Always thought there was money to be had without working for it…

I was the working parent and I also attended college courses trying to earn my A.S. degree in Administration of Justice. After a while, the money I brought in from my jobs and from my pell grants and student loans were just not enough for Wayne. He always wanted more than he had. I always signed over my paychecks to him and even got on Welfare too so he could have that money too, which eventually led to me being convicted on a felony count of welfare fraud. We paid the bills and then whatever was left, he spent on expensive toys for him, guns, drugs, parties, and new kitchen gadgets that he would use once and then put away. I didn't have a driver's license, so he had to drive me to and from work most of the time and if I wanted to go somewhere else, I had to either walk or ride my bike. Which after I had my first foot surgery, it became a little more difficult to get around. I had another foot surgery on the other foot a year and a half later.

I was raised with a totally different concept on life, but I tried to find a medium, so that I could have my peace of mind too. Some people still continue to question me about why I stayed with Wayne for so long. I can tell you that mostly, it was because I felt like I had no where to go and he was kind of like a bad habit, but I almost always could predict him.

There were times when the beatings and abuse would have what I have found out to be a "honeymoon period". Sometimes, those periods could last anywhere from 2 months to up to 8 months. With each beating, the bruises got deeper, the injuries became more painful and what dignity I had left was slowly, but surely beginning to fizzle away. There were so many people who knew Wayne and I in the community I now live in and to this day, there are still many who have their doubts of the kind of life I describe to you today. I can tell you that I was there, it did happen and I will live with those scars, both emotional and physical, the rest of my natural life. Just as my kids do too. My son is still a bit in the denial part of the loss of his father, but he too is learning that some of what his dad did even to him was not right and he knows that what his dad to me was definitely not right. No one deserves to be hit, not even once. As for my daughter, well she was so young when their dad died, but all she remembers about Wayne and I together was our fights and the screaming and the yelling and seeing her mom crying in her bedroom a lot.

I have been kicked, beaten, tied up, choked, strangled, shot with a b.b. gun, chased down the street with him behind me with a loaded rifle in his hands, tied to a chair and gagged while being hit in the head back and forth with a very large telephone book, hit over the head with many objects such as logs, glasses, fists, his boots and other foreign objects. He has broke my nose a few times, which I always made excuses when in public like I fell or was playing softball with the kids or maybe even getting hit in the eye with a ball of ice instead of snow. I have said I slipped and fell more than once and had even called in sick for my son when he was younger lying and saying he had bronchitis until his bruises healed up as well.

In May 1997, I had to have liver surgery because I had 4 liver tumors due to long-term use of birth control. The doctors believed that the one largest tumor was possibly life threatening because it was lodged on my hepatic artery. I was very scared to even undergo such a surgery because my outcome was not a very promising one. I had to do a living will and gave my brother all rights to my possessions, which Wayne was upset about, but I felt that my next of kin should be in control of those things and Wayne and I were not married. I stressed over what would happen to my kids if I did not live long enough to see them grow up. Would Wayne keep them from my family? Would he not allow my kids to even know or learn about my side of the family? He had always told my kids that my family was horrible and was nothing but no good alcoholics and bums. I just knew I had to get through this surgery. Wayne basically took my mom and I to the hospital and left. He told my mom he had bills to pay and things to do. I later found out where he ended up on that night. He called me at the hospital and yelled at me constantly that I needed to hurry up and get home because I had duties to do at home. He said that my surgery was my choice and that I did it, so I had to live with it. He didn't come and see me once while I was in the hospital except right after my surgery, but called me every night. I spent 8 long days of painful recovery in the hospital. I had a hard time recovering because they cracked my breastbone and my chest to remove the part of my liver. I lost almost 33% of my liver.

I also experienced a near death experience. I believe, while undergoing surgery, I saw somebody who said they were my guardian angel and they made me a deal. They would let me live to see my children grow up, but I had to agree that if Wayne ever hurt me again, that I would do anything I could to get out of that situation for good. Whoever said, "Be careful for what you wish for", obviously had been in my shoes before.

Our neighbor, who was a single and older man, was a pretty good friend to Wayne. He and Wayne did stuff together and just kicked it around the house drinking and hooting and having a good time like men do. He never hid the fact that he liked me though. I think that intimidated Wayne more than he let on. I, on the other hand, was too scared to even look at another guy. That neighbor was a very good friend to the whole family.

Approximately 2-3 weeks after I got out of the hospital, Wayne came home from one of his drug friend's house and I was just starting to be able to walk on my own. We had been given 60 days to move out of the house we were living in and I still had staples down my chest and stomach. Wayne and his mother expected me to do most of the packing and stuff. So I tried to do what I could. Then one night, Wayne came into the bedroom and got mad at me because I couldn't give him sex. He beat the living crap out of me that night. Then after he hurt me and kicked me a few times in my staples, he dragged me out to the kitchen and got his gun. He then told me he was going to kill everybody in the house because he didn't want us to see the Armageddon or some crazy thing like that. I was freaking out. I was not going to stand by and let him hurt my innocent children because he was so miserable himself. I began to scream at him until he went outside and got into his new Bronco that he bought with a fake name and fraudulent credit cards. After about 15 minutes, his mother started yelling at me and told me if I wasn't so useless, he wouldn't be so miserable. I just couldn't believe that she could say that to me after everything I had done for her and I was still trying to recover from the beating I had just taken. He threw me over boxes, into walls, punched me, kicked me and just beat me down like a dog. I urinated blood for 3 weeks after this episode, but he wouldn't let me go to the doctor for it. So, I finally went outside and when I found Wayne, he had a gun to his head and told me he just wanted these voices to shut up. He told me about these voices for a couple of years, but he was saying that these voices were becoming more prevalent to him. They were telling him to do terrible things to everybody. I managed to talk him out of killing himself that night.

Two days later, Wayne came home from this woman's house that he had been spending more and more time with and who was supposedly one of my best friends. He told me that it was over between us. That he had been seeing somebody else, but that I couldn't leave until I paid off all of his credit cards and bills. He didn't want his mother, our kids or anybody to know we weren't together anymore. So he would wait until everybody was asleep in the house and he would make a bed on the couch. He would get up before anybody got up and put the bedding away every day. I should have known that something was wrong then, but I just wanted out of the hell I was being forced to live in.

A couple of weeks went by and I got a job working at the local hospital as an Assistant to the Director of Nursing. Wayne was becoming more and more erratic and violent with every coming day. I also noticed that he was using more and more methamphetamine. I had only done it a few times after I had surgery. It made me sick, but he kept working me day and night in that house, I had to do something to keep up. He didn't care that I was tired and in pain.

Wayne began showing up at my work place unannounced several times a day, which made it very hard for me to perform my job. One day, he came and found me in my boss' office and ordered me to come outside to give him my paycheck. My boss told him that I was working and that he would have to come back at my lunch. Needless to say, that it only made him angrier. My boss, who had just recently got out of a violent relationship herself, noticed the signs right away and saw how scared I had become of him. After Wayne left, she closed her door and began to tell me her story and then told me to tell her what was going on at my home. Hesitantly, I told her about the violence, the abuse, the stress I was under and how afraid I was to go home that day because I knew I was going to get it for allowing him to be talked to by my boss like that. She then gave me a binder, which contained information on domestic violence, which is part of the protocol at the hospital, and told me to go to my office and sit and read the information. I was so scared. I had never told anybody outside of the house or family the details that I had told her. In the binder was a safety plan that I was to give to two people who I could trust and would know that if they got a phone call and I said just one code word, they would know what to do. Not knowing whom to tell. I decided that the best thing I could do was to tell the woman whom Wayne had been hanging out with, because she had always been a very good friend to me (big mistake). The other person I went to was our neighbor from the neighborhood we had just moved from.

This all took place about 2 weeks before Wayne killed himself. After I went to our neighbor, I began to break down before I could ever get anything out. He knew that there was something going on, but he never had any idea of how bad the fights were. He told me how he always heard Wayne yelling at me, the kids or his mom. He just wasn't aware that with the yelling and the screams, there were blows being thrown. I just remember looking up at this man and telling him that I had feelings for him for a long time, but I was always too afraid to show them. I knew I wanted out of the hell I was in and I knew that this man would put his life on the line to help my kids and me because he was a firefighter and put his life on the line everyday. He did. He was my prince.

After I had set up this safety plan with both of the people I had told, we began to meet at the woman's house because she lived across the street from the hospital I worked at, so I could just go over to her house at my lunch time. On one occasion a week before his death, she even helped me call an officer from her house. At that time, I told this particular officer about the abuse, the fraud, and how scared I was because Wayne's behavior was becoming more and more unpredictable and extremely scary. He told me he would see what he could do to help. I also told him that if Wayne ever knew I had talked to the law, I was dead meat. I told him about Wayne's involvement in a militia group and how against government he was. This officer told me that the story I was telling him sounded like something far-fetched. If he only knew, I also worked with another officer's wife at the hospital and decided that maybe he would listen to me. So I wrote him a note and put it in a sealed envelope and stamped it "confidential". Then I took it to her and asked her to give it to her husband as soon as possible. That very next day, he called me at my office and I told him a bit more about my story. He was the one who told me I had to stand up to Wayne and tell him I wasn't going to live afraid anymore before the law could even do anything more to help me. So, I took his advice and went home that night and did just what he said. I don't think I've ever been so afraid of Wayne before until that night. I remember shaking uncontrollably while I told him I wasn't going to live like that anymore. We weren't together, so why did I have to stay there? Why couldn't I just take the kids and me and move on and live a life where I didn't have to wake up every day hurting? I also told him that when he made love to me, it made feel like vomiting because he couldn't expect me to feel love for someone who continued to beat on me. He got so mad, he told me I could leave, but the kids were staying with him. I did tell him I was no longer going to live afraid of him anymore. I think I was hoping that there was somebody outside listening to us. He went downstairs for a little bit. I picked up the phone and had called our neighbor and told him how scared I was. Then the phone went dead while I was talking. The next thing I remember is Wayne storming back into the room telling me that I wasn't going to be able to call for help anymore. He tried to choke me. Then he let go. We fought for almost 2 hours that night. I found out later that when the phone went dead, my neighbor immediately got into his car and stood under the window and listened to the entire fight.

Wayne began to accuse me of seeing this man too. I never admitted it to him though. Not even the day he killed himself while he had a gun pointed at me. I knew if I ever admitted it, we all would be dead. It was okay that he was seeing somebody else, but it wasn't okay that I was because he said I was "his" property. I did not start physically seeing this man until after this night. It was just something that happened and at the time, neither of us thought that it would happen again. He knew there was no love between Wayne and I though.

The officer who had told me not to live afraid anymore had also told me because I didn't have any apparent bruises at the time I was telling him about the abuse or previous police reports, it was my word against Wayne's. Without any proof that he was acting erratic, it would be hard to prove or justify. I took some drastic measures at that point. My neighbor and almost lover at the time went to the local Radio Shack and bought me a voice activated mini tape recorder and a bunch of blank tapes. The 3 of us decided that I had to get some kind of proof as to Wayne's behavior and what he was saying to me. Oh my gosh, I still feel the adrenaline run through me when I think about this. I began to carry that recorder with me at all times when I was at home. Using the bathroom time to flip the tapes. I would give the woman the tapes everyday on my lunch hour so Wayne wouldn't find them. I had no idea what her motives were until later.

Still recovering from my surgery 4 months prior, I had hurt my back walking around so much at work two days before that horrible day and the doctor had given me prescription muscle relaxers. I remember sitting in my office before going home from work and thinking about how far I had gone to get out of this relationship and knowing that I couldn't turn back now. I felt very scared, but I was determined that I wanted out. There was no love between us anymore and I feared for my kids' future. Wayne's mother was going to have to be on her own because I couldn't do any of this anymore. I felt like the dead horse that had been beaten even after I had been shot. The hopelessness I felt was so overwhelming, but if I died trying to free my children, then it was going to be worth it to me. My son was already beginning to talk to me and treat me the way he saw his father treat me. My daughter was just a total bundle of nerves all of the time and I knew that couldn't be good for her either. I now know what it means when they compare a mother's love to that of a Mountain Lion and her cubs. They fight for their young even if they die doing it.

The morning of September 14, 1997 is a day of horror that I don't think my kids or I will ever forget. About 9 am that morning, the woman who I had been giving the tapes to called me and told me she had been listening to the tapes and strongly believed that something bad was going to happen to me and the kids and to get us out of the house. I kind of acknowledged her because when I had answered the phone, I had just woke up and Wayne had been standing over me…Talk about fear…I was feeling it welling up inside of me. I just told her I'd call her later. She started asking me if I was alone in the room and I told her no and that I would call her later and hung up. Never in the entire 12 and a half years I had been with Wayne had I ever woke up to him standing directly over me with a crazed look in his eyes. The night before this, we had talked things out and decided we were going to try to work things out, but I knew by the look in his eyes that wasn't going to happen. I tried not to act surprised by his actions and just looked up at him and said good morning. He just turned away without saying a word. I was beginning to feel panic build up inside of me. I decided because my back hurt so bad that maybe I needed a hot shower, so I went and took a shower, taking the tape recorder with me and making sure the tape was rewound and at the beginning. When I got out of the shower, I found Wayne sitting at his desk writing something. When I peeked over his shoulder, I saw that it looked like a suicide note. I asked him what he was doing and he got really upset and jumped up and told me to leave him alone. He then folded up this paper and went downstairs to give it to his mother. When he came back upstairs he had an envelope with my name on it. I just looked at him with astonishment. He told me to read it. I did and what I read still haunts me to this day. The letter read these words:

De Anne,
Let me start by saying that I have never been good at expressing my self verbally except in anger, and I mistakenly thought that anybody who really knew me knew that I was just pissed of or blowing off steam and would get over it. I believe that my anger and violence come from feelings of frustration with the fact that my life is going no place. Both in education and finances, and I thought that you probably knew that and understood, but I guess I was wrong. I also made the mistake of listening to you

when you used words like love, forever, and loyalty, these words come from your mouth not your heart. And I must say at this late date that I truly regret these mistakes, and feel that they were not worthy of the level of betrayal and the lengths you have gone to hurt me. Also let me say in the defense of this "monster" who was allways there picking you up and backing you when the world sh*t on you. Who was alwas ther when you sick of fresh out of the hospital. Yep it was me the "monster". Who allways was up front about who I was. So in closing let me say "life is a dance" and keep dancing.
Wayne

I wrote this exactly as he had written it. He wasn't very good at grammar or spelling. I got a copy of the letter he had given to his mother later. From the information I gathered after the act, I found out that Wayne had told his mother that he was going to kill himself that day and she called him an asshole and wrote him off. He also had waked my son up before anybody else that morning took him around the house to show him the items he wanted him to have. Then told him what he was going to do and that he wasn't doing it to hurt him or his sister, but to blame me because I had broke up the family.

The other letter that he had given his mother that morning read these words:

September 14, 1997
It is my wish that the remains of my body be creamated and held onto until a time that a member of my family of blood relation can afford to personally go out to sea on a fishing boat and scatter my ashes personally. Do not leav it up to any one else or a company.

Furthermore it is my wish to be laid to rest intact there are to be none of my body parts donated.
Wayne Joplin
Aka
Jon Peterson

Jon Peterson was the name he had been using for about a year prior to his death.

As this day went on, it felt more like a nightmare that had come true. The night before, I had dreamed I was standing in the street where I lived and was looking at my house with flashing lights and sirens, but when it came to seeing a body, there was no face in my dream.

After I had finished reading the letter that Wayne had given to me, I just looked up at him and told him to come sit down on the bed so we could talk. That's when he pulled a 9-mm pistol out of the back of his pants and started waving it around. He started telling me that he wanted me to admit to him that I had been having an affair with the neighbor. I kept telling him no it wasn't true. He told me that I should go to him because we belonged together and that he knew that he could give me a better life than the one he had given to me. He also said that he knew that he could take care of the kids and give them the love he never was able to show. I just looked up at Wayne. I began to tell him that he needed help and it was the kind of help that I couldn't give to him anymore. He started yelling at me and told me that the only help was the family and the family was the center, but I had destroyed that center. He then pulled out wads of some kind of plant and began to chew it. He told me it was foxglove and that he had been eating it all morning. I knew what foxglove was because it was something that he had learned from hanging around with the militia group. It contained digitalis, which is supposed to make you have a heart attack. He then began talking crazy to me. He told me he had been drinking heavily and then he went to the closet and laid out his best suit that he wore to his grandmother's funeral. He said he was going to go call his brother and see if his brother wanted to go to church with him. I knew then that something was terribly going wrong. Wayne had always professed himself to be an atheist. I told him to sit down so we could talk about whatever it was that was bothering him. He told me that he wanted to hear me tell the truth about my affair because he had been feeling guilty about sleeping with the woman who I had thought was my friend. I still told him that I didn't have an affair. You have to be married to be considered having an affair. That's when he started crying to me, which I had never seen him do before. He told me that he had planned on us getting married that New Year and that I could be married under the name he had been using for the past year. I told him that I had decided that I didn't think I wanted to marry him anymore until he got some real help. He then said he needed to use the restroom and tried to hand me the gun to hold for him. I knew what kind of man he was and he was trying to get my finger prints on that gun, so I held out the sheet on the bed and told him to put it there. He decided that maybe that wouldn't be good. He started to tell me how he always dreamed that He and I would go out in a blaze of glory like Adolph Hitler and Eva Braun. I got chills that made every hair on my body stand up. He then began to tell me how there was foxglove drying for me too in the smoker downstairs. I was beyond panic at this moment. He then got up with the gun and went to the bathroom.

I picked up the phone and just pushed a memory button and decided whoever answered the phone was going to hear my code word. It turned out to be the woman I have described, I remember her answering the phone and I just told her, "Oh my God, he's got a gun and he's going to kill himself!"

The next thing I knew, Wayne came spinning around the corner and fired off two shots at me. In all the years I had lived with him and all of the times he had butt stroked me with his rifle or pistol whipped me with his pistol or just plain put the gun to my head, he had never fired a shot before. The first shot missed me. The second shot, I felt graze through my hair and it hit the phone, which was in my hands. Pieces of the phone flew up and hit me in the face. I was deafened by the sound of the shot. I was holding my face where the pieces hit me thinking I had really been shot. He started yelling at me to tell him whom I called. I told him it was her and he then grabbed me by my hair and threw me down the stairs and told me to go get on the phone and call her back because he didn't want anybody to try to stop him from what he was about to do. He then told me that he had made arrangements to avenge his death and that my lover, my friends and me were all going to be taken care of. He then told me how his intentions were to kill the kids one by one, then his mother and then me and then him. I still feel extreme terror when I begin to talk about this part.

He threw me into the counter in the dining room and told me to pick up the phone and call her back. I picked up the phone and there was no dial tone. The phone line had undergone some shock, evidentially at being shot at moments before. I kept hitting the button until finally I got a dial tone. I dialed her number again and when she answered she told me the sheriff was on his way, I told her what he told me to say and then she talked to me trying to keep me on the line. He grabbed the phone from me and called her a traitorous bitch and hung up on her. I saw my opportunity to get his attention away from everybody at that time. The sliding glass door was open a little and he had moved out of my way. I ran with everything I had. I ran out the door and out onto the street not looking back. I could hear him behind me though for a few seconds. He was yelling at me and telling me to come back. I saw the sheriff coming up the street and I just kept running barefoot towards his car. He saw me and pulled over and told me to stay behind his car. (He later told me that he had seen Wayne chasing behind me with the gun). This particular officer was on the verge of retirement. I noticed as he began to approach Wayne that he wasn't wearing his vest. When I turned back towards my house, I saw Wayne go in the sliding glass door and then he came out the front door onto the porch. He put the gun to his head. I ran towards the sheriff to tell him not to go near Wayne because he would shoot at him. All I remember was the Sheriff turned to Wayne very calmly and told him to put the gun down and that they could talk things out. Wayne replied, "No Jerry, you don't understand, I have to do this." Then he pulled the trigger.

Our kids and his mother were standing in the doorway, the sheriff was about 5 feet away and I was right behind the sheriff. When I saw Wayne's feet go up in the air and his body fly off the porch into the bushes, I thought to myself that was the most helpless I had ever seen Wayne. I remember saying the Lord's Prayer over and over to myself as I ran out that door. I remember feeling relief when I saw him pull that trigger and then everything went black and numb.

When I woke up, I found myself sitting in the back of a sheriff's car, shaking, weeping and thinking about the tape I had in my pocket. I gave the tape to the sheriff. The next thing I thought about was my kids. Were they alive? Were they okay? I went to run towards the house, but his body had not been removed yet, so the sheriff wouldn't let me go until his body was gone. I remember standing there, watching the paramedics put a sheet and a hood over his head. What was white was blood stained red now. It was horrible. I started telling the other officer I wanted a cigarette, which I hadn't smoked for years. The next thing I saw, were about 4 packs of cigarettes from by-standers being tossed at me.

When I was finally allowed to go into the home to see my kids, my son went hysterical, which I found out later from him that he thought I was trying to make him go see his dad. He kicked me and hit me and told me he hated me. Wayne's mother told me that I better get out of the house before she killed me. The officer that had escorted me into the house, grabbed me and escorted me a bit forcefully out of the house at that time. I thought that the terror was over finally and after we all got through this rough time, we would all move on. I was so wrong about that. When I thought things couldn't get worse, they did.

The neighbor, who had become more than that, and I had been put into victim witness protection for 5 days, until the sheriff could sort out the whole mess and figure out if Wayne's threats were real or not. All I remember thinking was where my kids were and were they really going to be okay. I knew that my son acted out of anger and fear. I was worried about my daughter too; she was only 3 and a half years old at the time. It wasn't until that evening that the traumatic shock settled in on me. I went to the woman's house for a little bit afterwards, but then went with my boyfriend when he showed up. While we were at the motel where the sheriff and victim witness had placed us, I went to take a shower. I remember looking down as I was washing and seeing that there were spots of blood and brain tissue all over my legs. I broke down and started to cry and scrubbed myself raw with a brillo pad. I felt like I couldn't get clean. I was shaking uncontrollably and vomiting non-stop. He finally scooped me up and placed me in his car and took me to the hospital. The hospital staff was very discreet in letting me in because Wayne's family was still in the building, so they let me come in the back door. The doctor gave me some strong sedatives and some other medication that he said would help with the shock. I ended up being treated at least one more time that week.

Of course I took a week off from work due to the stress I was undergoing. I didn't have enough leave time saved up yet because I was still new to the job, but I did take the bereavement leave they offered to me. When I did come back, the first thing I had to do was handle all of Wayne's admission records that had DOA written on the top of them. I thought I was going to be sick after that. I tried to push myself through the rest of the day. I did find out that the in-laws had taken custody of my kids during that week too. I was okay with that as long as I knew they were okay. I had no place to live except with this woman and I was teetering at losing my job because I couldn't concentrate on anything. I don't think it was helping that Wayne's sister-in-law kept coming to my work either.

On September 24, 1997, I was working in my boss' office, when I heard my name being paged over the loud speaker to report to admitting immediately. My boss just kind of looked at me and said that this was a job and no visitors while I was working. I told her I would go see who it was and tell them to come back. When I went to the admitting room, and then the same officer who escorted me out of my house grabbed me the day Wayne died. He told me that there were some folks outside that needed to speak to me now. I asked him if I could go tell my boss, but he said that it wasn't possible at that time. He grabbed my arm and wouldn't let me go. When I got out into the parking lot, I found myself surrounded by a few other officers. Some were in plain clothes and some were in uniform. One of them I recognized as being my probation officer from the county I was on probation with for the welfare fraud. My probation time was almost over with too. I was then advised that because I was on probation, I was subject to a probation search of my belongings and areas I lived. I think one of the hardest things was when I had the officer go back to my boss' office with me and tell her what was going on, so I could leave. She tried to tell them I would lose my job if I left, but they didn't care and I had to go. The first place they searched was where I was staying at this woman's home, which was also Wayne's drug connection. I was totally scared because I had my daughter visiting that day and I didn't want her to see the cops with her mom again. They wouldn't let me go in first to tell her that everything was okay though, so I had the woman I was living with take her to her neighbor's house while they searched the home. They gave me the routine pat down and then took my belongings and dumped the boxes upside down. After they were done there, they made me get into their vehicle and they took me back to the house where Wayne had killed himself. I had not been in the house since that day.

I finally asked these officers what it was they were looking for exactly so I could maybe help them find it. They told me they were looking for any more evidence of Wayne's fraud and anything that would indicate me using any other names. They found some old bills with my name on them and then they took my diary that my grandmother had given to me before I went into the Army. I should have known at that time that wasn't all of what they were thinking, but I didn't have my wits about me just yet. I was still in shock over Wayne's suicide and losing my kids to his family until I could get back on my feet.

When we arrived at the house where the suicide occurred, I asked the officers if they could at least allow me to go through the other door, because I didn't want to step foot on the porch. There were still blood splatters all over the place. Fortunately, the officer that was there the day Wayne had died spoke up for me and told them to do it for his sake too.

They did. We had not finished unpacking from our move as we had only lived in this house for about 3 weeks, so stuff was still in boxes all over the house. The officers took me upstairs and made me sit on the couch after they removed the cushions and made me sit while they searched. I can not believe the mess they left the house in when they finished their search. The search took about 2-3 hours total. I was in even more shock at some of their findings. They had found a letter that Wayne had written to Timothy McVeigh explaining how he supported his cause and such. They also found many catalogs of Wayne's that had chemicals and supplies to manufacture his methamphetamine. They even found some powders in the house that they said were weak versions of "speed". I knew that he had made the stuff a long time before, but didn't know about how he was try-ing to do it again. They also found the foxglove he mentioned, in the smoker downstairs which wasn't there when they checked the day of the suicide. They found some of his written plots on some of what his plans were at bombing government buildings and such.

At one point, the officer who had witnessed the suicide asked me to come into the bedroom where I had sat the day he fired his shots at me and kind of show him what I was doing and where I was sitting. When I did, they found the bullet shells. He let me keep the one that had grazed my hair. I still have it and keep it as a reminder that I never want to go through this again.

After the search was complete, they let me go back to work. I told my boss everything that was going on and she was in as much awe as I was. A couple weeks later, I was let go from that job, but put on the rehire list. They just said I had too much going on and had to get it together before I thought about coming back. I told them, "Thank You". Then when I went home from work that day, the woman who I had been staying with, had her friend whom was her landlord, give me a letter that said I had to get out that night. So I called the neighbor, who was also becoming more of a boyfriend to me every day, to come and pick my things and me up. The officers had advised me that I could not leave town until they said I could. The events from then on changed my entire life and the way I view friends and people.

I spent that winter being treated for Post-traumatic Stress Disorder, severe depression and just plain out suicidal thoughts and tendencies. I had my daughter come and visit on my good days when I could handle it. I just didn't want her to see me in the state I had been in. My sister-in-law, who was also caring for my kids, called me all of the time and was telling me how Wayne was dead because of me. My son wanted nothing to do with me because I was living with this man and she told me that I was being investigated for Wayne's suicide and the investigators felt that I had forged those letters that Wayne wrote. I'm left handed. That was one thing that most people overlooked until then.

I continued to have poor relations with the sister-in-law, but began to have a relationship with Wayne's mother, who was living with the brother-in-law who was caring for my two kids. She would call me when she was alone and tell me how miserable she was about her life and everything. She began to forgive me in her own twisted way over my relationship with the man who I was living with now.

It took me 6 months before I was in a state of mind to be a mom again to my littlest one. My son, on the other hand, still was very angry with me and refused to visit with me or anything. My counselors told me the one thing that showed him I loved him more than life itself was by showing him my unconditional love. I awarded only the uncle legal guardianship of him in April of 1998. I never gave up any of my parental rights. The only reason I did this for Jason was to prove to him that I did love him and that I would give him his time to heal and when he was ready, he knew where he could find me. I never gave up hope that I'd have him back with me someday. Regardless of what anybody told me about my decision.

My parents weren't very supportive towards me after the suicide for many reasons. Mostly I think they were hurt by me. I denied on several occasions the abuse when they questioned me about it. My father was so upset by me allowing my son to stay with his uncle. The only people I had for support during this period were my counselors, some of my past co-workers and the man who I now lived with and was falling in love with.

In June of 1999, I was dragged through the ringer. I had to go to an Administrative Hearing with the state and the county I reside in. The whole thing was over the evidence that the officers had taken from me after Wayne's suicide and they were trying to pursue charges on me for committing Welfare Fraud. Unlike the first time I was convicted, I had some money to hire an attorney and not a public defender this time. I also didn't have to live afraid of Wayne anymore. So I was able to plea Good Cause for my commission due to the severity of the abuse. Although I had no police reports I felt I had enough people who would come forward and tell the truth. The prosecution side subpoenaed Wayne's mother, his brother, his sister-in-law and the woman I had lived with right after the suicide to testify against me. It was probably one of the longest hearings even the judge had endured. I was able to get the doctor to raise my medications for the depression until all of this was over with. For 7 hours, I sat and heard their side of the story and then some of the people I had told my attorney to contact were able to also testify. This included my counselor at the time, one of my former co-workers, my new boyfriend and past neighbor and some of my other past coworkers. A month later, I received the decision in the mail. The judge had deemed by me showing proof of one time I had been admitted into the Emergency Room for a severed finger, that Wayne's mother had lied about taking me to, her testimony was thrown out. There were also other elements of evidence that were proved to the judge in this matter and she said I had Good Cause for committing the fraud. The rest of the decision was that I make payment arrangements for the amount that they felt I was responsible for after they recalculated all of the amounts in dispute and giving me the work allowances for those months and years.

Two months later on August 9, 1999, Wayne's mother passed away. My son had found her keeled over from a heart attack. He was very close to her and so was my daughter. I had mixed emotions about her death and I still do. She was the reason for Wayne being the way he was, but she had her good qualities too. I also respected her because she was my kids' grandmother.

I began to make payments on the $2700.00 that the county and my attorney had recalculated me owing in August of 1999. I continued to make those payments religiously, because I was also trying to work on my previous conviction being expunged in another county.

On February 13, 2000 my one true dream came true. The man who had put up with me and whom I had grown to become very much in love with proposed to me and gave me a ring. I did accept and as I am writing this, we are actively making our plans for this coming spring.

On February 14, 2000, just when I thought things were starting to look up, I was arrested for the previous charges of welfare fraud. After I spent about 5 hours in jail and spending $1000.00 of his money, my fiancé bailed me out. My attorneys were livid over this act. We fought with the county over their actions and on April 28, 2000 all charges were dismissed for good.

Since then, I have been working on regaining my sense of who I am and where I want to be in the future. I have been working for the U.S. Forest Service for the past 3 fire seasons as an Information Receptionist and this past season I worked as a Relief Fire Lookout. I received my driver's license in April of 1998. I received my EMT-1A certification in December of 1998, which I use for my job mostly.

I think the best thing I can say that has happened now is that my son and I are now spending lots of time together and he has learned to accept this man as his future stepfather. He still resides with his uncle who lives 8 miles away though. His uncle has also gone through divorcing the woman who was my sister-in-law and he too is now engaged to be married soon. There are so many things I am thankful for now and I love living and I love the feeling of being loved.

I still have nightmares that haunt me sometimes about that day of the suicide. I still deal with many ghosts from my previous life with Wayne.

My son, my daughter and I have really worked hard to get where we are at today. We still continue to see the family counselor from time to time and I continue to see my personal counselor as well for some of the more intense issues that I have to deal with. Life is good and I still deal with bouts of depression, but not as often as before. As for the suicidal tendencies, I no longer feel that it is the answer to any problems. I always tell my friends who are going through bad divorces and wish their ex-husbands dead, that they are easier to deal with when they are alive. I still feel that I have a ways to go in my recovery of the nightmare I lived, but I think I'm over the hump now. Please, if there is anybody who is reading this story and you know somebody who may be in the situation I have described, don't turn your back on him or her. Be their friend and give them the support they need. They have to feel secure with their support system before they can get the strength to battle their fears and get out alive. Thank you for listening.

~DeAnne Deane, California

A Vow

February 1992

I was a good mother.
I was a nice woman.
Struggling to return to the Self I'd abandoned.
Trying to do it right, no mess, appear normal, appear together, try harder.

VIOLENCE struck!

I woke up in an instant. For the first time in my adult memory I could SEE.

Foolish, foolhardy, ignorance and ignorant. We attempt to kill one another all the time, without thinking or feeling.

Numb to Grace
Numb to God
Numb to Love

Calling strength weakness and agreeing it is so. Nonsense beyond belief. Name calling at every turn, heaping guilt and fear, calling it love, believing we are right.

We following standards set by a system that destroys, not builds, in the name of God! What God? Whose God?

I choose! No More! No More! I vow to live by my awareness. It is not neat! It is not ordered and tidy by the pre-set standards that will not recognize it!

It too So long to grow up! I AM No Longer Afraid. I'll Live and Stand for Non-Violence.

~Nan Diebels, California

Please Carry Me

July 2000

I am so tired
It's now about three
Up all night thinking of you
Won't you please carry me?

I carried you
With love deep inside
Every movement I felt
Filled with great pride

You were the answer
To my special prayer
Entrusted by God
To give you the best care

As I walked on the beach
You holding onto my head
You were the "Sunshine on my shoulder"
You were two then, (you can't be dead!)

How could anyone kill you
You were loved by all
You turned your back and he hit you
Caused your death, made you fall

Over twenty-five years
We were best of friends
Though my heart is now broken
The love never ends

I miss our long talks
Your laughter and wit
It's too much to handle
And I want to quit

How can I go on
Please tell me how
My life feels so empty
No more happiness now

It doesn't seem fair
To share all this pain
With the others I love
Could I be insane?

The doctor says no
I am deeply bereaved
It just seem too long
That I have been grieved

I am getting better
I keep telling my friends
Putting myself back together
Tying up the loose ends

It seems my life started
And revolved around you
I find myself wishing
That it would be through

But then I realize
God's plans are different for me
Why? Why? I keep asking
Maybe someday I'll see

I have to keep going
I'm not finished here
"They" can't keep us apart
I feel you are near

Each day somewhat brighter
With thoughts of your memory
And I'm starting to feel
That you are carrying me

I will carry you with me
Until my life on earth ends
When we are together in heaven
Where my heart finally mends

Dedicated to My Super Son, Bill
Love Forever and Ever, Your Mom

~Deb, Florida

A Homicide Survivor? Who Me?

March 1994

What do you do when someone that you love is murdered? How do you go on? What is the "right way" to handle the changes that you will face? The answers to these questions are not taught in any school. No book or class or TV show prepares you for a loss like that. We take for granted that it can't happen to us, cocooning ourselves with a false sense of security in life. We read about someone else's tragedy in the newspaper or see a clip on the news and shake our heads. "How horrible for the family." But it doesn't go any further than that. It doesn't touch us. It ALWAYS happens to "*other people*". On a beautiful spring Saturday in March of 1994 I became one of those "*other people*".

My dad was gone. Just like that. In the time it took my mom to say, "your daddy's been murdered. He was beaten to death." My life as I had always known it was over. Why was he murdered? Because he had a couple of hundred dollars in his wallet? Because he tired to help what he thought were two young women in need? Because it was his time? It's been six years since he died and I still don't know the answer to that question. I know who murdered him: Two males, ages 21 and 17 and two females, ages 16 and 14. I know that the motive was robbery. What I don't know and can't understand is why those four felt the need to kill him. Why couldn't they have just overpowered him and taken his money? Why did they have to beat him to death with an ax handle and leave head and facial wounds that were so severe that I almost couldn't recognize him?

Nine months after his murder I faced my first Christmas without a dad. In case that wasn't hard enough I spent the day before Christmas Eve in a courtroom, facing the four that took his life. They got lucky. The system showed them mercy and offered a plea bargain. My dad had no such offer when they killed him in cold blood. As I sat up on the stand and tried to explain to the court what they had taken from me I looked in their eyes. Did I see remorse? Did I see sorrow? Did I see an ounce of compassion? No! I saw pure hatred from one, boredom from two, and a look that screamed "oh man-I can't believe that I got caught" from the fourth. The judge thanked me for my time, listened to the other statements from the family, painstakingly explained how many years, months, weeks and even days the one being sentenced was facing in prison banged her gavel, and it was over. He was led off in handcuffs and I was left to cope. Weeks later, when the other three took their turns in front of the judge, I couldn't be there. My doctor wouldn't allow it (I was eight months pregnant) and my heart and soul couldn't take it. So how was I supposed to continue on with life? How could I possibly go on with business as usual? The four of them were in prison BIG DEAL! My dad was in the grave. There is no time off for good behavior in the cemetery. They sentenced my dad to death and he had no court of appeals, no Governor to plead with for clemency. Business as usual would be usual again.

Over the years I've gotten my fair share of "we're sorry to inform you" letters from the Board of Paroles. An appeal here, a plea for clemency there, my heart being torn apart again and again. It never gets easier. I see the state seal on an envelope and start trembling. Luckily they are never successful but it doesn't help me to face the next one and the one after that. The straw that almost broke my back was an email that I received this year, a week before Fathers Day. The name was vaguely familiar. The subject line was "Your Web Page". Since I get comments about my Survivors site frequently I didn't think a thing about opening it. It took a few lines of reading for it to hit me…the letter was from the father of one of the girls that murdered my dad! The room started spinning, the contents of my stomach started heaving, and I felt like I couldn't breath. This man started off his letter nicely enough. He spoke of how he had come across my page and how sorry he was that I had lost my dad, and from there it went downhill. He told me how wrong I was about his daughter's participation. He claimed that she had known nothing of what the others were planning and how she had lied to the police in her confession. He asked me to forgive her and talked about how it wasn't really her fault.

The root of her problem, according to her father, was being molested when she was 12. Doctors, hospitals, and tons of money couldn't seem to help her. She started running away, hanging out with the wrong crowd. Yes, I felt compassion for her and what she had faced. No, I did not think that it was a good enough excuse to murder a man. Being a victim of crime doesn't make it ok to hurt others. He said that she's very sorry and is turning her life around in prison, being a "model inmate". YAY! My dad stays dead no matter how well she behaves herself in prison, no matter how sorry she is. She gets out in five years. He'll still be dead. My first thought was to write him back and rant and rave about the animal that he raised. My friends and loved ones talked me out of it. No amount of reason, of facts, is going to make this man look at his child as a killer. In his eyes she's just as much a victim as my dad was.

How to survive when someone that you love is murdered. There just isn't a manual out there with the steps listed out. In time the nightmares go away, your appetite comes back, and you can go through an entire day without crying. The pain even lessens but it never goes away. A part of you dies the day someone that you love is murdered. You can never think of who you lost without the manner of their death being the first thing in your mind.

Has any of this made sense to you? Will you put this book down and think, really think, about what it means to be a homicide survivor? Will you have a better understanding of the pain that we face every day? I hope so. If this has helped one person understand, even a little bit, then it has been worth it.

In Memory of her father, E.W. Strother III

~Kim Strother Jones, Georgia

MEMORIAL FOR SEAN ALAN BURGADO

May 1997

This memorial is written for my nephew. It is believed that on the evening of Monday, May 19, 1997, Mr. Sean A. Burgado was murdered shortly after he arrived home from work at around 9 p.m. He had been beaten and shot through the chest. Sean was pronounced dead on May 21, 1997. Sean was born on June 7, 1969 and was 27 years old when he died.

Apparently, Sean was dead two days before the body was found. Sean did not report to work, so his boss called the neighbor to see why he did not go to work. The neighbor called for Sean, and when he did not answer, he opened the door and found Sean dead with his face down in a pool of blood. He still had his work uniform on. They quickly called the police.

When Sean was an infant, I was asked to be Sean's Godmother. I had taken Sean to the Catholic church to be baptized. Sean was such a beautiful, bouncy, healthy baby. Subsequently, I did not see Sean for many years. However, when Sean was 24 years old he went to stay with my mother (his grandmother). I got to see Sean once again-he had grown up to be such a handsome lad, and I was really proud of him. I loved Sean's smile.

Financially, Sean was not doing well, but he was determined to find a job and work hard for survival. He came to work with me at my home doing cleaning and some minor office work. We would clean together and chat about family life. Sometimes, when he was short of cash and needed money, he'd say, "Aunty, I need to make an "IOU"". I would loan him the money and he would reciprocate in house cleaning. Sean was good at keeping track of the hours he owed me. Sometimes, I'd say don't worry-you can pay me back later.

Sean graduated from High School in June, 1988 and went into the armed forces. He worked at Pasty baking cakes and breads for many years. Sean was a hard worker, and at times, went to work very early in the morning at approximately 4 a.m. Subsequently, he got a better job working at an Elderly Care Center in the cafeteria as a baker. He was happy because his new job was a State job, and it was a steady job. He would have made his one-year anniversary working there in a couple of weeks just before he died. Sean loved his job and loved all the people he worked with. Everyone, loved Sean at the job, and the boss said Sean took pride in his job. He brought new ideas from his old job. To earn additional income, he was going to work an additional job in another elderly center doing the same thing (baking).

Sometimes Sean and I would go to have dinners at a fast food restaurant or inexpensive restaurants, and we'd chat about his goals. First, he wanted a job and a good automobile, and secondly, he was going to find a girlfriend. He had one, but it didn't last. We talked about going to college to get a degree-he was very optimistic.

I remember going on a picnic one day in the park. I was rushing to get something done, so we could relax at the park. He'd say Aunty Lori, you need to relax, you work too hard!" "Just kick back and look at the beautiful ocean and enjoy" He was very funny at times.

Sean lived alone in a little studio with many neighbors very close by who loved him. They invited him to their home for dinners which he enjoyed. He was so appreciative when invited for a family meal. His favorite meal was roast beef, and his favorite cake was the chocolate delight cake. I remember how Sean loved to talk about love. He'd say "Aunty, love is so valuable". It does not cost anything to give love. More people should not only tell one another how much they love each other, but they should show how much they care. He'd say I believe in encouragement and people should encourage one another. We always shared big hugs and ·I love yous."

He had two cats whom he loved and took good care of them. He also loved to play with my mother's dog. He loved music and loved to listen to the Survivors. He loved sports especially football. He use to visit his friends Ronnie and Annie and while there, watched sports with them on TV Sean had an old automobile which gave him trouble all the time, and Ronnie would help Sean repair it.

I last saw and spoke to Sean in February, and at that time, I gave him a big hug and took a gift for him. I assured him I would be there for him if he ever needed me for anything. He wanted a favor and I did as told. I did not dream that would have been the last time I would see Sean. I loved Sean dearly. I now have only wonderful memories of Sean.

Sean looked forward to life he had many goals and dreams. Just when Sean's life was coming together-someone takes it away. Unfortunately, Sean is not able to achieve those goals now. We don't know who would want to hurt Sean and take his life. Sean would not hurt a flea. We don't know why, we don't like it. It feels wrong. We pray that justice be brought to the person or persons who took my dear Sean's life. It is a nightmare to me-my heart aches for Sean. I cry a lot and there is a lot of anger at the person who killed him.

~Lorraine "Lori" Ornellas, Hawaii

THE BREATH OF SPRING

June 2000

I can hear the tick of the clock. Silence is behind the tick. My tears seem to never end. Pain fills my days, the ache in my heart as the pieces fall, forever broken. Darkness is all that I can see. My Crystal is gone. I can't hear her voice. I strain to hear it, but it fails me. My arms ache to hold her, I feel so empty. Her beautiful face and her smile forever gone. I'll never heal from this. Nothing seems to comfort me. I pray as best as I can, but the words just won't come. God help me I feel so sick, the pain is searing my being. The sky should be black. The earth should be rumbling and rain pounding the ground. These tears are for me, I just don't understand. I have searched my soul and cannot find comfort. I know God's word, I have read and re-read it. My heart still weeps and can find no comfort. I know Crystal is much happier and in a beautiful place. This does not comfort me. I am selfish I want her here with me. I want to hear her laugh. I want to see her do her "silly" little things. I want to hold her and tell her how much I love her, how much I need her. How blessed we were to have her as our child. I want to tell her how beautiful she is, not just on the outside, also in the inside. I feel so guilty. I didn't keep her safe. Please dear God let her know that I beg her forgiveness and let her know how much I love her. She was my child with the tender heart. She would do whatever was asked of her. Crystal's smile would lift any heart. Crystal was the sunshine of my days, the breath of spring in darkness. She was my beauty. I was truly blessed when the Lord gave me Crystal. The angels truly kissed her. She was so giving and had such a tender heart. She would cry when someone was hurting, even if she didn't know them. Crystal was a wonderful daughter, sister, aunt and mother. Crystal loved her children more than life itself. She often boosted of their accomplishments and held them tenderly in her arms as she thanked God for them. When Crystal held her children you truly knew that the Lord blessed us as well as her children to have her in our and their lives. I am so very proud of her. Crystal was always a "Daddy's Girl" but I loved her from the time I knew she was under my heart. My life is truly empty without my Crystal. Crystal, Mommy misses you more than you'll ever know. My heart will never be the same, it is forever broken my beauty.

~Diana G. Abney, Kansas

3 Years Gone

October 1997

It's hard to believe that nearly three years have passed now. The wound left by Anastasia's murder remains open, and still bleeds. It happened almost three years ago, but it happened just yesterday, and it will happen again tomorrow.

I was not related to her, not by blood nor by any legal bond. All the same, we were family.

I knew she was someone special the first time I met her. She was two and a half at the time, and her intelligence and self-awareness were remarkably evident, even then. As she grew, her interests grew apace. Her curiosity never waned.

Anastasia and her sisters quickly became my "adoptive" nieces, and when I spoke of them to others, I frequently forgot to include the "adoptive" in my reference. I thought of them as my godchildren (and odd term to use, considering that Anastasia was and that I remain religious skeptics) and myself their mentor; more than that, they were among my closest friends. Anastasia, being the oldest, sought my help and counsel more often than her siblings. As a teen, she would call me on the phone just to chat about everything and nothing. We talked of politics, philosophy, science, school, family, anything. I would share many of my interests with her, and she made many of them her own in time. I cherished those conversations as life lessons for both of us.

I can recall so many memories of her: helping her with her first arithmetic lessons, and watching that epiphany spring from her as she suddenly grasped the mysteries of addition; trying to teach her parallel parking many years later, and feeling her frustration as she tried to master the skill; seeing that jump-for-joy happiness when we got her computer set up for her sixteenth birthday, and the fun and frustration that followed; helping her launch her first web page, as she taught herself the intricacies of the Internet, and surpassed her mentor in several areas.

But with whatever I might have given Anastasia, she gave me a gift of immeasurable value: she shared her life with me, and invited my participation. There is nothing that I could have been given her to match that. I am incalculably richer for because of her life, and indescribably poorer because of her death. The lessons of the heart she and her sisters have given me are worth more than anything I could have given or taught any of them, and I cannot imagine what my life to now would have been without them as part of it.

I remember her joy when she graduated high school in June 1997, and of my own feeling of gratitude for having shared it with her. It may well have been the happiest day of her life, with her whole life in front of her, and a world to conquer. Later that summer and through the fall, as her relationship with her boyfriend soured and fell into an on-again, off-again pattern, I was among those who thought it was just a matter of time before they would quit seeing each other altogether; little did we know the horror that awaited them both.

Anastasia and I had many arguments over her responsibilities, as she struggled between adolescence and adulthood, often depressed, frequently full of anger and frustration, but also full of love and a great capacity for joy. I always told her that she was a work in progress, and the last words I said to her, in a phone conversation two nights before her murder, were "I love you"; her last words to me were "I love you too". I will treasure and carry her words with me to my grave.

And those words are not said often enough. If we learn nothing else from this hideous loss, we should learn to tell all of those we love just how we feel, not just now, but every day, as a habit, because Anastasia has very painfully reminded us all just how fragile and precious all our lives are.

I am told that "closure" is a phantom concept, that people you love die and that you have to move on. They will never be back, the gap left by their passing will not be filled, you will always miss them, but still you must go on. And we have all tried to do that for Anastasia, remembering her without obsessing.

However, the circumstances surrounding her death and the subsequent actions (and lack of action) by our local police force have made it difficult to even do that.

We never expected closure from her murder, but we did expect justice, or at least an honest attempt by authorities to gain that. Instead, we have witnessed almost a textbook case of police incompetence, indifference, and arrogance, compounded by the complicity of several local governmental agencies and local media to help keep that information from the public.

Anastasia was murdered by persons unknown by a gunshot wound to her face on the night of October 22, 1997. Her body was found in a cemetery in a county in Missouri the following morning, and the body of her boyfriend, Justin, was found elsewhere two days later, killed by a shotgun blast. The County Sheriff's Department, which is investigating Anastasia's murder, still refuses to link the two deaths.

The officer in charge of the investigation originally considered it a suicide pact, despite many obvious clues disputing that theory, and only looked at a more likely suspect (possibly in both deaths) after receiving information from two sources, both friends of Anastasia, implicating another acquaintance. He still did nothing for nearly a month, asking one of the sources (a minor at the time) to gather further information for him. The source's mother immediately called the officer to register her disapproval of the officer's methods, and her demand that he not involve her child any further.

Within days, the officer went to the home of one potential witness mentioned by the two sources, and disclosed to that witness the name of his source, and within hours that information was passed to a suspect. The source was immediately subjected to harassment and threats, and the police made no effort at protection.

What the officer did was not just a mistake, but under Missouri law was a crime. Missouri Revised Statute 610.100.3 states that "if any portion of a record or document of a law enforcement officer or agency, other than an arrest report, which would otherwise be open, contains information that is reasonably likely to pose a clear and present danger to the safety of any victim, witness, undercover officer, or other person; or jeopardize a criminal investigation, including records which would disclose the identity of a source wishing to remain confidential or a suspect not in custody; or which would disclose techniques, procedures or guidelines for law enforcement investigations or prosecutions, that portion of the record shall be closed and shall be redacted."

In basic English, the law makes it a crime to disclose the identity of a source wishing to remain confidential during an open criminal investigation. It is a Class A misdemeanor with a $1,000 fine and a three-year statute of limitations. This information was given in writing (along with a written statement from the deputy in question admitting that he disclosed the name intentionally) to the County Prosecuting Attorney, but he has refused to return phone calls on the matter (except to say he is still "considering the situation"), while the statute of limitations slowly ticks away.

Meanwhile, a complaint was filed through the only channels allowed in County, an agency known as the Office of Human Relations and Citizen Complaints (OHRCC for short). It took more than a year to bring the complaint to a conclusion, including a time when the agency closed the complaint on verbal request of the Sheriff's Department without bothering to notify the complainant. OHRCC eventually held a hearing, but stacked the rules of procedure against the complainant (among others, refusing her the right to question respondent, refusing to exercise their power of subpoena, and attempting to restrict her ability to summarize), and did so on the advice of the County Counselor, who was representing the Sheriff's Department in the hearing. OHRCC made no decision, wasting several more months in the process, and is currently being sued by some of Anastasia's family and friends for violations of Missouri's Sunshine Laws in the course of their proceedings.

The family has tried to gain some media attention to this abuse of power, but the local media has been scared away as well. Reporters would talk to the family about the lawsuit and/or police crime, and then be pulled from the story by their editor following a call from the County Counselor's office.

Not that there has been no media coverage at all. Two months after Anastasia's murder, a *Star* reporter approached Anastasia's family and friends, saying she wanted to do a story on the murder. We all welcomed the opportunity for some publicity to our case, hoping it would draw more public attention. We had no idea that this person came into our midst as an assassin, her goal to destroy Anastasia's name and reputation. She asked loaded questions, and drew her own conclusions from otherwise innocent answers. When it became apparent to the family that she was intending a sensationalized account that would directly link Anastasia's Goth interests to her murder, we took exception. She assured us she would do a "fair" story; so much for journalistic integrity.

Yes, Anastasia was interested in the Gothic subculture. She enjoyed literary, musical, and fashion tastes in common with Goths. Many, though far from all of her friends in the last year of her life were Goths. But she herself couldn't be described as much more than a "weekender" Goth, as she occasionally wore the Goth "uniform" of an all-black ensemble, but would just as often wear much more colorful stuff. (It should be noted that the reporter thought the black ensemble was "proof" that Anastasia was deep into Goth, yet when it was pointed out to her by an interviewee that she herself was wearing an all-black ensemble, she simply said, "Oh, but that's different.") Anastasia once in the summer of '97 dyed her hair black, but she'd been dyeing her hair a variety of colors for a few years by then, and her family did not take particular note, nor did they need. By the end of summer, this particular fashion phase had faded, and she returned her hair to its natural chestnut color. She enjoyed such nouveau-Gothic literary interests as "Sandman" and musical ones as The Cure, but she also enjoyed Terry Pratchett and The Beatles, as far from Goth as one could go. Justin, as described by friends and family, was only peripherally interested in Goth, and made no manifestation of it, other than his naturally jet-black hair and his predilection for sporting a black jacket.

The *Star* reporter cared not for those facts, and leapt to her own conclusions. When Justin's family listed a large and varied list of authors that he had found interesting, she picked Anne Rice, author of the "Vampire Chronicles", as the only one to mention. (God only knows what she would have done had she known that Anastasia had actually met Anne Rice at a book signing.) She quoted a CSD Captain as saying "It wasn't unusual for these people to hang out at cemeteries," never making an effort to learn whether they actually did, or whether this was a generalized and possibly prejudicial statement on the part of CSD. It is still unknown whether the Captain was referring to Goths in general, the Goths of Anastasia's acquaintance, or to Anastasia and Justin directly; if it was the latter two, we have yet to see any evidence to support that idea. The story entered the realm of Alice In Wonderland, where Anastasia and Justin were guilty of Goth (as if that were itself a crime), and the *Star* tailored the evidence to fit the verdict, even grossly misrepresenting the Gothic subculture as badly as she had Anastasia's and Justin's lives. (That story can be found on the News Accounts page.) We had hoped for a human-interest story, but were "treated" to one worthy of The National Enquirer.

Anyone who had read that story and did not know Anastasia personally could easily draw the conclusion that she and her boyfriend "dabbled in the macabre" and could even be led to believe that they may have somehow "deserved" their fates. No matter what their real or imagined flaws might have been, neither of those young people deserved to die, and both definitely deserved better than this wholesale trashing of their lives by someone who knew little and cared less for them.

Anastasia and Justin both deserved so much better than the fate that befell them three years ago, and their memory cries for a justice that the police, government and media have all failed to give them since. Her family still suffers her loss every day, and her memory cries for justice.

~Patrick Rock, Kansas

You Should be Getting on with Your Life

April 1996

"You should be getting on with your life" says a friend of mine. I am always amazed by that statement. When people say that to me I want to SCREAM at them, but I don't because I realize they do not say it to upset me, so I resist the urge to scream at them. What is it they really want from me? For me to be the same personas I was before my son, Devin, was murdered? NO that will never happen. Part of me was murdered with him and I will never be the same. Shot in the head three times is not something you ever "get over" or "forget"!

Don't they know that just getting up every day is "getting on with my life'? I work part time, help my 22-year-old daughter in any way I can. I cook, clean, iron, walk the dog and pay the bills.

Do they want me, in their minds, to get on with my life by forgetting my dead son, to quit grieving? I wonder if they really mean "your making me uncomfortable", so please change. Is it because I talk about my murdered son? When Our nightmare happened in April of 1996, I would lie in bed and wonder how I was going to live. In my mind I was screaming "God help me, I can't do this." I watched my wonderful husband of twenty one years cry everyday, our seventeen year old daughter struggle with nightmares and with now being an only child.

Should I forget Devin's handsome face with the twinkling brown eyes, his dark brown hair, his teasing and entertaining personality? Should I forget how he loved pizza and buffalo wings, how he played baseball, his love

53

for his cat, Ponch? Do I forget how he cried when his grandma and grandpa died unexpectedly?

I have already "gotten on with my life." I can smile-I can even laugh. Life has a different meaning for me now. Behind my everyday mask, if you care enough to look, look into my eyes, there is another story of grief, pain, sadness, anger, lost hopes and lost dreams.

Yes, I have "gotten on" with my life. I go to my friend's sons' weddings now and I watch a part of life that I so desperately want and will never have. I watch new life beginnings for other peoples' sons. No dreams and hopes for our son now. I now hope and dream of surviving this soul pain everyday.

Perhaps my friends should say "I'm happy to see you standing. How do you do it? " That would give me the opportunity to say, "I get my strength from God, my husband, my daughter, but most of all, Devin himself." His voice in my head saying "Mom, you can do this. Go for it. Remember me and live life the best way you can."

I take comfort and peace in remembering everyday of the 20 years we had with Devin.

To do anything but to live life, would dishonor Devin. So, I have "gotten on with my life" bit I am taking my son, Devin, with me.

Mother of Devin

~ Debbie O'Brien, Maine

KEVIN

March 1985

"I am here to inform you that YOUR SON DIED last night."

The words are still ringing in my ears even though they were spoken 15½ years ago. I can still see the very sterile Marine officer standing there, telling me that my beloved son Kevin was dead.

"No, that is not possible, I spoke to him last night and he was fine, in good spirit and excellent health. Why are you telling me this," I screamed at the man. My eyes moved behind him and I saw the Chaplain. My heart started pounding and I thought that I was going to faint from fright. I realized that something awful had happened. I tried desperately to gain control of my emotions. Did Kevin die from a sudden illness or was he killed in a car accident? What could possibly have taken place in the few hours after I spoke to him on the phone?

It looks like a homicide.

MURDER.

I looked out of the window at the glistering snow. The first day of spring had just arrived. The sun was shining and my life, as I once knew it to be was over.

Death had come to my son, not as the dark hooded specter with a sickle in his hand, no death had come in the form of another Marine with a combat knife that viciously stabbed my 21 year old son to death.

Kevin was dead and he died on his sister's "Sweet 16th" Birthday. My family would never be the same. I was falling apart, I wanted to die so I could be with Kevin. Dad could take care of the girls, but Kevin needed me. How could anyone kill my son? He was such a good person. So loving and caring. And yet someone took upon himself to do this evil deed.

A week after the murder, when the authorities were done with my son's body, they shipped Kevin home, across the country for his final journey. I had sent him to California. A healthy young, handsome boy, and they returned him to me in a flag draped coffin.

"So sorry about this, our deepest sympathy."

My son died alone in his barrack room, 3,000 miles from home. In a place where he felt secure. In a place where he belonged. But he wasn't even safe there.

The following months became overwhelming. Details of his death surfaced. It was ever so gruesome. I started to go into a state of pretense. It was all a lie. Kevin was alive and somebody was simply lying to me. How could such an active boy die? Ever since he started to walk, he was forever in motion. So busy. Always doing things. Sometimes things he should not do, but he was a very normal kid.

He filled our home by just being in it. It is quiet now. His music has stopped and his room is empty.

How could one person leave such a void. My heart is still aching and a big part of me is missing. I know that I have two girls and I know that they need me. But I need my son also, I miss him every day. I had so many hopes and dreams for him. In one horrible moment they were forever gone.

When Kevin was murdered, the killer took not only his life, he took away our future. To watch him grow into manhood, to make something good of his life. To have the pleasure of becoming grandparents to his children. The joy of him being an uncle to his sisters' children.

I try not to waste my time thinking about the creature that took my son from me. I have enough to deal with.

I am walking on. My journey is not over, I am a different person now, I am a grieving mother. I want my tears to dry up. I want my heart to be happy again and I want to look into that handsome face grinning back at me and give me one of those wonderful hugs again.

~Chris, Maine

In Loving Memory

June 2000

This poem was written on June 12, 2000, 3 days after my friend Jason and his girlfriend were car-jacked, kidnapped, and driven to a golf course, where they were each shot in the head. I have this for you to read for one important reason; it has always been my dream to write a book. Jason and I used to write together, he was the only person I trusted to read what I had written. One of the last things he said to me the night he was murdered was, "I will be with you when you write your first book." I have held these words in my heart since the day it happened, and I will hold to them. I will write a book. When my friend informed me about this book, I immediately wanted to send my poem. I think it is an excellent idea, for an excellent cause. I hope that many will read the book and can understand that we have all faced a tragic loss.

Sincerely,
Katelyn Demers

In Loving Memory of Jason
February 15, 1980 to June 9, 2000

We can not see you
We can not touch you
But we know you are there
Of course you are smiling,
Dancing on clouds, wishing on stars
Watching us think of you and remember you
There are no tears where you are
There are no enemies
Only the best of friends, like those you left behind
Take them skiing
Write them poems
Dance with them, make music for them
Make them as happy as you made us
We miss you
We miss your laughter, your energy, your dreams
But they will never be far from our thoughts
Remember that we will always remember you
For who you were
Who you are
And who you will always be

We love you, Jay
And will miss you always
May the stars that shine ever so bright look over you
As you look over us

~Katelyn Demers, Massachusetts

MY FOREVER FRIEND

June 2000

"If I were to give you one piece of advice, it would be to look to the future, for the past hurts too much"-Jason, 2/15/80—6/9/00

Do you miss me as much as I miss you? Jason "Jay" was my first date, my first kiss, my first boyfriend. More importantly, he was one of my best friends. He helped make me the person I am. He showed me how to take risks, how to share my life with someone. Because of him, I found a part of me I never knew existed. Together we went skiing, fishing, and on rides to Providence merely to get hot dogs. As I came to know the real Jay, I realized that, although we were not meant to be together, he was my soulmate-"my forever friend." No matter how many foolish arguments we had, I invariably knew that the argument would be forgotten, that no grudges would be held, that he would always be there for me. When times were good, we celebrated. When times were bad, he made them better.

But how can this get better?

A tragic twist. Everything was finally perfect. It was a storybook ending that none of us expected. Through a series of unexplainable events, Jen, Kate, and I were all good friends again, and to celebrate, the three of us decided to surprise Jay by showing up at the club together. There, the four of us danced and hugged and laughed about the past, the present, and what was to come for us in the future. *"This is so cool,"* Jay exclaimed, giving the three of us a bear hug. *"I can't wait to hang out with you all together!"* Unfortunately, time was not on our side that night, for much too soon it

60

was time to go. When the clock hit 1:00 am, the music ceased, and our flawless night drew to a close as we exchanged hugs and goodbyes.

But how could we possibly know those would be his final goodbyes?

Everyone believes tragedies like this can only happen to other people. Jason was not sick. There was no accident. He was not being pursued. Someone knowingly and willingly stole his life from him, from us, because he (the killer) simply had nothing better to do that night. Jason was only twenty years old, and he had so much to live for. As his family and friends search for answers we find that there are no answers, not a word to give us the slightest comfort. The commotion has calmed down for the time being, but I dread the day the trial begins because everything, and much more, will be opened again. Reporters. Photographers. Policemen. Why can they not leave us alone to grieve?

When Jay left, a piece of me went with him. Sometimes it hurts to breath because I miss him so much. Indescribable feelings of emptiness and pain lurk within me. At the age of twenty, I have never been more afraid of the dark than I am now. Sometimes I lay awake at night, staring into the darkness, waiting for morning to come so I can feel safe again. Classes, work, and friends are my only escape, for when I am alone, I often think about him. What if we had not convinced him to go to the club that night? What if those men had just robbed him and left him alone? What if I had been there? What if? What if? What if? Thoughts race through my mind until I break down and cry. Tears are calming until my memories trigger again. A vicious cycle.

Words cannot express feelings. I wrote in a journal several years ago that when I die, Jay was someone I would like to have speak at my funeral, yet only four months ago I instead had to speak at his. On the eve of his funeral, I sat at my computer, frantically searching for just the right words to say to let everyone know exactly how much Jason means to me, to all of us. Finally, tired and teary, I sat down and sorted through letters Jason had written me, for his writing could always make me smile. There I found a card he sent me for Valentine's Day two years ago, and his words combined all of my thoughts about him into two perfect sentences. He wrote to me, "You will always mean the world to me, and the world is a big place. So when you think I am not there, not listening, not with you, I am." These words I used to say my final farewell to him. I only wish he had been here many years from now to read them for me.

~Robyn Lussier, Massachusetts

Carmen Amicae Meae Carissimae

October 1997

For us, death used to be a joke.
We'd pretend to be dead.
We'd make-believe it was glamorous;
It was desirable.
Then it was.
It was fun, it was interesting.
It was black and smoky
And tasted of coffee and cloves.
Our hum-drum lives were spiced up
By the stories of our "friends",
The stories we ourselves lived with them.
We were wise to be cautious,
That life wasn't to be ours yet.
It reached out, yearning for us.
We let our guard down;
It reached again and snatched
You away from me.
I tried to pull you back,
But it wouldn't loosen its hold on you.
Every time I pulled, it pulled harder.
After a while it let up, thinking
You wouldn't escape;
But you began to sneak out.

Once you were nearly free from it,
It grabbed you from behind
And hurled you right into
The center of its dark chasm
From which none can escape.

~Daniele Lynn Fields, Missouri

MEMORIES OF A HOME

July 1996

Christmas Eve twenty-seven years ago a soft snow was beginning to fall the first time I crossed the threshold into the brightly lit dining room of a couple who would later become my in-laws. The noise was deafening, people and children seemed to be everywhere. The children, all sizes, were running and playing, the TV was blasting out above the din of voices. Quite a change for someone used to small reserved family gatherings.

Once in the dining room, a small kitchen straight ahead was crammed with people, food and drink. Dishes were piling up everywhere; no one seemed to notice; trash was overflowing. To the left in the dining room a fire was crackling and popping in the large living room. Everyone seemed comfortable and enjoying each other's company. My family gatherings had always been quiet and polite.

Later, several gathered in the dining room drinking and eating special baked cookies, brought out from secret hiding, while playing penny poker late into the night. Cigarette smoke began floating in a haze becoming a fog as the game went on for hours. Others stretched in front of the TV hooting and hollering for their favorite team, while others were asleep, warm with full tummies. How they could sleep was beyond me. The most my family ever let lose the night before Christmas might be an annual highball followed by the annual offering of a piece of chocolate from a Whitman's Sampler, followed up by a quiet game of dominos.

Standing in the archway of the dining room one stepped down into the large living room. A door to the right let to this couple's bedroom. The door was closed; off limits I learned and so it remained for the next twenty-five years. I only entered the room by invitation a few times over the years, mainly when I needed a quiet place to call my aunt in order to be heard above the resonant din.

These Christmases and other family holidays would continue on for years in this same fashion up to the forty-ninth year of marriage for this couple, now my in-laws. Then, one day, like a page out of Truman Capote's book, "In Cold Blood," our lives changed forever. There in the bedroom that was always a secluded area of the house the couple were murdered execution style by a man who had sat in prison planning this vile crime. Upon his release, he put his plan into action, which would change our lives forever. Thrown into the throngs of court, Lawyers, estate work and the day in day out shock of what happened to our idyllic life we huddled.

What would happen to this big old house that held so many good memories for all followed by the tragic memory of what last took place inside those walls? The house would have to be sold, but who would want to buy a house where a double murder took place? Our answer came one day, after a long day at court listening to the horror of the last moments of their lives which were so hard to digest. Later we gathered at one and another's homes; we felt better if we were together. A sister stood up after eating pizza and drinking beer, while at the same time discussing murder and how we felt about the death penalty; a subject most of the group had hardly gave a moments thought to before the tragedy. "I want to buy Momma and Daddy's house." Most in the group thought, how could you live there after the terrible tragedy of what took place there in their special room? One in the group voiced the thought, "How can you live there and expect your family to after what happened?" Calmly the reply came, "I am not going to let ten minutes of bad memories override forty years of happy memories. I want us to be able to still gather at the house in the tradition Momma and Daddy began." What a wonderful way to look at the old house full of memories.

And so it was, my sister-n-law, Angela bought the old home place. Today, when someone pulls up front to the house, they see a beautiful tiered flower bed the length of the house. The weathered old wooden front door has been replaced by a cranberry colored steel door with etched glass and double lock. As one crosses the threshold, the old carpet has been peeled back revealing the old wooden floor polished back to life. Straight ahead the kitchen has had a face lift any woman would appreciate. New cabinets hang, one with a pink stained glass making it the focal point of the room. The one thing remaining constant throughout the refurbishing is the big window where one can cast their gaze out and occasionally see deer stepping daintily through the field close to the woods. Turkey still swoop in and gather to gobble and eat in small groups. To the left, in the dining room one sees the fireplace in the big living room is still there, but flanked with new dark cranberry tile. Stepping down, the old pounded beige carpet has been replaced by a lighter cranberry carpet throughout the house. The walls too, have undergone a subtle change from finger-printed dirty white to hushed pink. To the immediate right once stood a hollow door where an unthinkable tragedy occurred inside; it now opens into a large archway bright and sunny. A play room for young grandchildren to gather in, perhaps a den or library in years to come. Angela truly made lemonade out of what was a huge and foreboding lemon. The old house full of memories has certainly become a painted lady ready to continue her role of creating memories for generations to come.

~Karen Sparks Long, Missouri

Remembering Kyle

January 1997

Kyle Gulledge was born December 22, 1958, in Ogden, Utah. His life ended on January 6, 1997 by a bullet through his back while preparing dinner in his kitchen in rural Ray County, Missouri.

Kyle was the son of Mary and Robert Gulledge, the last born of three. He was the brother of Keith Gulledge and Julie Wade, the father of 14 year old Bryan Gulledge. He was a grandson, a nephew, an uncle, and friend of many, but especially Big Al Morgan, Chris, and Suzanne Scott. Kyle loved riding his horse, fishing and hunting with his dogs. He particularly admired eagles and had started a collection of them.

Kyle's father was in the Air Force and stationed at Hill Airforce Base near Ogden, Utah. When Kyle was one year old I moved back to Kansas City, Missouri with him and his brother and sister. We lived with my parents until his father was discharged a few months later. We moved into a house in Independence, Missouri. Kyle fell in love for the first time when he was five and asked if he could marry the littler girl and bring her home to live with us. To marry and have a family was always his goal. He met the girl he would marry while in high school and they were married not long after graduation. His son was born about five years later. They had purchased a house in North Kansas City but when it was destroyed by a fire they purchased a farm in Ray County, Missouri, a few miles south of Excelsior Springs. It was a very remote location and his wife was never very happy there. Kyle was a heavy drinker and that also caused problems. He did enter a rehab facility for a few weeks and joined AA by the marriage ended eventually. He retained custody of his son for the first few years but when the son expressed a wish to try living with his mother Kyle let him go.

Kyle lived alone except for every other weekend when his 14-year-old son visited him. He had been married for 13 years then divorced for 6 years. More than anything he wanted a happy family life. He was terribly lonely and depressed and almost desperate to find someone to share his life. He thought he had found that woman a couple of years previously. She moved in with him and lived there for 1-½ years. They were planning to be married. However, it was a troubled relationship from the beginning. They fought and she moved out. Then, that summer, Kyle lost his job. This was another crushing blow for him. He was still seeing the woman on and off but began drinking heavily causing further problems. She told him if he would get counseling and help for his problems she would come back. He agreed and she made an appointment for him at a mental health facility where he attended group therapy for two weeks. He was diagnosed as manic depressive and put on medication. After two weeks he was released to a therapist named Randy for additional counseling. Randy agreed to sessions at Kyle's home because Kyle had lost his drivers license due to the drinking. At this time the woman he had been with told him she wasn't coming back and wanted to end the relationship.

Kyle confided to Randy how lonely he was and how much he wanted to meet someone. Randy told him he knew three women he could introduce to Kyle; one a 22 year old he had treated in the past, Angela. He told Kyle how nice and sweet she was and he would interested in her himself if he wasn't engaged.

Kyle agreed to meet Angela and early in November 1996, she called him and they arranged to meet in a public place, along with Kyle's son and Angela's 4-year-old daughter. They saw each other every day and Kyle enthusiastically described her to me along with his high hopes for a permanent relationship with her. I cautioned him to take his time, to not rush into anything. I was uneasy because of Kyle's problems and I knew she had problems of her own. I didn't think Randy should have introduced two people he was counseling. Nevertheless, two weeks later Angela and her daughter moved in with Kyle. He brought her to our house for Thanksgiving and we met her and her daughter. The next day Kyle called me and was anxious for my opinion of Angela. There was little I could say after one meeting except she had seemed sweet and polite. I didn't tell him that my granddaughter, his niece, told us she believed this woman was evil and wanted us to warn Kyle.

Angela worked nights and had been using a baby-sitter but now, since Kyle wasn't working, he took care of her daughter, did the housework, cooking, etc. When Kyle asked Angela for a little help with the utility and food bills, she was outraged. She began to spend more and more time sleeping, going to work late, then missing a lot of work. She wouldn't help with the child's care or any of the chores at home. Kyle said she was "flipping out" over everything and nothing at all. She was fired from her job and things worsened between them.

About a week before Christmas Kyle told me he was going to ask Angela to leave but wanted to wait until after Christmas for the little girl's sake. He also told Angela he thought they should part after Christmas. She became very angry and began screaming and hitting him, throwing canned goods and such from the cabinets. She said she was leaving and taking these things with her. When Kyle put his arm around her and tried to calm her, she kicked him hard in the groin. At that point he threw her to the floor. She then calmed down and decided to stay the night. The next morning she packed and moved out.

Shortly after moving out, Angela went to the police and filed an assault charge against Kyle. Two weeks later she called him and begged him to meet her at a store under the pretense that her daughter missed him and wanted to see him. When Kyle got to the store he was surrounded by police and arrested on the assault charge plus driving with a revoked license. A court date of January 14, 1997 was set and he was released on bond. He made an appointment with his attorney for January 10, 1997 to discuss the charges.

Kyle's birthday was December 22 and it was our normal practice, since he lived about 75 miles from us, to celebrate his birthday at the same time as Christmas because all the family gathered at our house then. However, that year I felt like I really wanted to have his birthday celebration on the 22nd. He was so pleased and kept asking me why we had changed plans that year and I told him it was just something I wanted to do. He told his friends Big Al and Chris later how much he appreciated it and how pleased he was. I was so glad later that we had done that.

On Saturday, January 4, Randy, the therapist called Kyle. He was upset and told Kyle there was something he needed to tell him but couldn't. He said if Kyle could guess what it was he would say yes. Kyle asked him if it concerned his arrest or something in the past. Randy said no, it hadn't happened yet. Kyle couldn't guess what it was and he was very concerned about it.

I began trying to call Kyle on Tuesday, January 7, to see if he needed a ride for his appointment with the attorney. His sister, Julie Wade and myself tried calling all week without success. I was really worried because I knew he wouldn't drive himself anywhere. But, my husband kept telling me to quit worrying, he was probably staying with one of his friends. On Friday, January 10, I called his attorney to see if he kept the appointment and was told he hadn't shown up. That appointment was so important to him I knew something was wrong. Julie and her son, Danny, picked up a couple of Kyle's friends who lived in his area and went to Kyle's house. Danny entered the enclosed back porch and looked through the back door leading in the kitchen and saw Kyle on the floor and there was no doubt that he was dead. They believed he had committed suicide because he had threatened to do so in the past. They called 911 from a cell phone and reported a possible suicide. When the detectives and coroner arrived it was determined to be a homicide. Kyle had been shot through the back, the bullet being fired from the front porch through a window in the front door which was in a direct line to the kitchen. Kyle had been standing there preparing his dinner. He had been dead since the previous Monday

night. The killers then entered the house and ransacked it. Nothing was
taken except two guns from a rather valuable collection. Julie and the others were detained for hours at the scene, having to wait in their cars in
freezing weather. Neither was she allowed to call anyone to tell us what
was going on. Finally, after it had been hours since she had left home I was
getting frantic. I called Kyle's house and the phone was answered by a
detective. I questioned him but he would tell me nothing and I knew at
that point that Kyle was dead. I think he sensed my panic and when I
asked to talk to Julie he said she was outside and would have to call me
back. Very shortly we received a call from Danny and was told of Kyle's
murder.

The following Monday, January 13, a major case squad was formed and
began their investigation. They received a call that day from a woman who
had seen the news of Kyle's murder in the newspaper. She told them that
Angela, Scot and Richard had been at her house the previous Monday
evening and they discussed killing Kyle. They discussed how to do it,
which one would do it and to get a gun. It was decided Richard would do
the shooting and Angela said she knew where to get the gun. She knew of
a pickup truck that had a rifle in the cab. They wanted the woman to go
with them but she said no, she would keep Angela's daughter while they
went. She said she didn't believe they would really go through with it.
When they returned they told her that they had not killed him.

Also on Monday, the 13th, police received another call, this one from a
woman in Warsaw, Missouri. When Angela left Kyle's home she went to
Warsaw and stayed with her grandmother briefly. Then she met Scot and
Richard, who were living with Scot's girlfriend and mother. They invited
her to move in with them. She did and the three began plotting Kyle's
murder and were telling friends and family they were going to take off on
a trip soon. After Kyle's murder the three fled to Ontario, California. Scot
became afraid of the other two and called his girlfriend and told he what
they had done and wanted her to get him some money or plane ticket so
he could come back to Kansas City. He was to call back the next day to

find out if she had gotten it. The girlfriend's mother called the police and told them of the call and they went to her home and put a tracer on the phone. When Scot called the next day the call was traced to a pay phone in Ontario, California and the three were arrested there and the extradited back to Ray County, Missouri. They were all charged with first degree murder and armed criminal action and the prosecutor said he would ask for the death penalty for Richard who, it was determined, was the shooter.

Scot agreed to testify against the other two for a reduced sentence. Subsequently, after many court appearance and trial postponements, all three pled guilty to second degree murder and armed criminal action. Richard was sentenced to two 30-year terms to be served concurrently; Angela was given two 29-year sentences, concurrently and Scot received two 20-year sentences to be served concurrently. They are required to serve 85% of their sentences before being eligible for parole. When that time comes we'll be there armed with hundreds of petitions to keep the locked for their full terms.

This senseless act has devastated Kyle's family and friends. Our lives will never be the same because a piece of us has been torn away. There is never any closure for the survivors of murder. We just have to learn to live with it and try to make some sense of our new lives. Being there for other survivors, listening and trying to help them is one way Julie and I are trying to make something good come of this tragedy. We all love and miss Kyle fiercely and think of him constantly. We've learned that this world we live in is full of monsters and the monsters are the only ones that have any rights.

~Mary P. Gulledge, Missouri

Reckless Horseplay is Murder: Joshua Eugene Hedglin

March 1997

The first time I saw Joshua was on October 30, 1978. He was the most beautiful child I had ever seen. I have always loved children and been drawn to them but not like this one. I fell totally in love with Joshua right away, I prayed day and night for God to give me the opportunity to be this child's mother. On December 4, 1978 a miracle happened, my prayers were answered, I became Joshua's Mom. Everything was right with the world.

Joshua was so smart he learned very quickly and was so inquisitive he was always busy exploring his world. He hardly ever cried as a baby. By five months he could say Da Da, La La (love you) and Ni Ni (night night). By eleven months he was walking, I was so proud of him you'd think no else child had ever walked or talked. I was lucky enough to be able to stay at home with Josh while he was young. It was a struggle to make ends meet but it was so important to me to be there with Josh so "Dad" took on two jobs. Josh and I did everything together. We took long walks and when it was snowing I'd bundle him up and set him on a sled and we'd still take long walks and look at the world around us.

When Joshua was three we moved to California to see if we could build a better life and Dad wouldn't have to work two jobs and he could begin to spend some time with Josh. Well it was an even bigger struggle but we did manage to make it on one job. The first time we took Josh to the ocean he was so excited to see all that water. As we drove on the pier he squealed with delight "look mommy there's stirin up boats." Josh what are stirin up boats, his reply was look right there mommy see there stirring up the water! He loved to watch the seagulls and the seals and of course he loved the water finding seashells was a favorite treat. We spent many hours during the day riding the bus around San Jose just looking at the town sometimes we'd stop at the "big mall" and sit by the skating rink and watch the kids skate, he loved it there.

Before I knew it was time to start school. The first day of school was on his fifth birthday, he thought that was about the best birthday present any kid could get. Now he began to grow so fast. But living in San Jose poised too many problems with a young boy wanting to explore the world on his own with his own friends. When he was six we moved to Red Bluff, California. In the northern part of the state. A much smaller town, soon he had many friends and was off exploring the world with his own friends. I missed the time we spent together but I was so proud of him and happy to see him growing so independent and having so many friends. In the fourth grade he made it on the honor role. But the kids would tease him and call him bookworm, although he never cracked a book, it just came easy to him. He was reading at the tenth grade level and could spell any word you could think of. He didn't like the kids calling him names so to compensate for it he became the class clown. Soon he found he could make people laugh and he loved doing that. I began a journal for Josh that Christmas, a collection of poems and thoughts and dreams for him. The opening page was: If I could give you one thing it would be that the world disarm it's bombs and lay down it's guns, drugs would be forever gone and the world would learn to live in peace without violence…

When he was thirteen we moved back to Missouri, where our family began. Here he would be safe. After a difficult adjustment time things began to settle down. Josh made lots of GOOD FRIENDS. Although the teenage years were trying, it was nothing unusual. He had many friends to the house for hours of fun, playing Nintendo, jumping on the trampoline, talking on the phone, just hanging out. Sleep-overs with his friends. He spent many hours with his friends at the skating rink. He finally realized a dream from when as a child we sat in the "big mall" and watched kids skate for hours. He loved to play baseball and football with his friends in the field by our house or soccer in the field by the college but his favorite thing was Hockey at the skating rink with his friends.

Sixteen was a difficult year for him, his best friend committed suicide that sent Josh into a tailspin but he seemed to recover although he was never the same as we all know we're never the same after losing someone we love. He went frogging with his Dad one day and stumbled over a young man who had went to the lake in our neighborhood and took his own life. This to affected him deeply, as it would anyone. In the few short years between twelve and sixteen, he had lost six friends to suicide.

Shortly after his friend's death, Joshua met a girl. He was so happy when he was with her they were a good match. He came alive again. He was that old mischievous young man with the crooked smile again. Whenever he wasn't working at Sonic he was with her. He graduated from high school at seventeen. What a bitter sweet time that was, I was so Proud of him yet so sad because it was the beginning of really letting go. Little did I know just how far letting go would take me.

He joined the Army after graduation and in a week he was off to South Carolina with his best friend. Unfortunately they were separated then, his friend in one platoon, Josh in another. Try as they might they never had the opportunity to see each other except for one brief moment at a concert on Fourth of July 1996, during basic training. They missed each other by days. When on leave, Josh's leave was over when his friend's was just beginning. In less than a year, Josh began to hate being there in the Army. He hated being around the guns. On several occasions he called to say I'm afraid someone will shoot me. Some of these guys don't know how to handle a gun. I want to come home. I want to go to college and become an art teacher (he was a great artist). So that's just what he did.

On February 25, 1997 he was honorably discharged and home where once again we thought he was safe. In two weeks he had gotten a job and had enrolled for the fall session at MU. He was once again a happy young man with the crooked smile. Though his girlfriend and Josh broke up during Basic Training, they remained good friends and there was still a twinkle in his eye when he spoke her name. He met a new girl.

It was on March 16, 1997 that the world stopped spinning. Josh went to pick up his girlfriend and spend the day with her. As he went out the door he called back to me BYE, MOM I LOVE YOU I'LL BE HOME AT 5:30. He would be bringing her home at 5:30 for dinner. On his way home he stopped off at another boy's house, it was there that fate spun it's evil web. This person (I'm trying to be Kind) was playing with a shotgun. There were several kids in the room; the parents were not at home. The sixteen-year-old boy was pointing the gun at each of the kids, they each asked him not to point the gun but he continued to do it anyway. He pointed the gun at my son's head, his girl who was sitting behind him pushed the gun away and asked him to not point the gun at Josh. He brought the gun right back this time aiming at Joshua's chest. Joshua asked him "Is that gun loaded?" the answer "well let's find out." In that instant of total stupidity and ignorance and with blatant disregard for human life, my son died.

At 5:35 the doorbell rang, I remember thinking, well get set for another practical joke but when I went to the head of the stairs I saw my Husband standing there looking so lost and as white as a sheet. There was an officer standing in the door asking if we were the parents of Joshua Hedglin. I remember thinking well you know we are, but in that same instant I knew why he was there. My mind screaming no don't say the words, I won't listen but still hearing the words coming from my mouth IS MY SON DEAD? You see I already knew, he didn't have to tell me, an hour before for some reason I could not identify, I became so cold and I knew something was horribly wrong but I didn't know what yet. But I now know what it means when someone says your blood runs cold because that is exactly what happened. I always knew when he was in trouble.

Somehow we got through the funeral arrangements, I remember it being so dark and not really being aware of what was going on, something inside just took over. It was like being outside your body looking down on strangers watching them make all these decisions and going through the motions. My mind remembers that week but my heart does not believe it was real it had to be a really bad nightmare and I have to wake up. Wake up is just what happened a few weeks later I found myself sitting on the ground in the cemetery, the darkness seemed to be broken up by the bright sunlight forcing it's way through the darkness. I remember the first thoughts were, what am I doing here, whose grave is this, did I lose my Dad, Oh, no this is my son's grave but how can this be. It can't be, Not My Son.

A year later we have learned more and felt more pain and betrayal than any parent should have to. We never got to say goodbye, one minute he was walking out the door the next it is 18 hours later and he is laid in his casket. I never held my boy in those last hours. I never saw him in the last hours, he was whisked away to the mortuary and that was it. It was over and I was supposed to accept this! Since everyone knew my son there was no need to identify the body but I would have liked to had the privilege of holding my sweet blue eyed boy one last time and to say goodbye with him in my arms.

We have learned how unfair the justice system can be. Though the boy was under house arrest for four months he seemed to just go on with life. Had friends over to his house etc. Still went to work with his friends. Finally after seven months the judge sends him to a detention center for one year, not enough for my son's life but at least a little justice, in December comes another blow, he is released from the detention center, free to start a new life after serving only three months.

Somehow after three and half years we have managed to survive. I don't know how except that we just keep waking up each morning and do whatever it takes to make it to the end of the day. Most days are still filled with tears and pain, and I doubt that will ever change.

One of my hardest things for me is the fact that someone could actually hurt my child in such a despicable way. The perpetrator walks away from this death with no scars, no remorse, but we as the parents live with a daily pain etched so deep in our hearts it can never heal. For a very long time I lost my faith and was very angry at God. Time has brought me back to God and my faith has been one of the strongest ropes in the last year. A year ago the depression and the pain of losing my only child became more than I could bare and after taking an overdose and waking up in the hospital I found my faith once again. I know in my heart that God was not at fault for this death and that God was there that awful day he came and held my boy gently in his arms then took him home where he would feel no more pain. I know deep in my soul that we will be together once again. I feel my Son in the cool embrace of the wind, I see my son in the brilliance of the sunlight, I feel his love in the warmth of summer sun. I hear his soft voice in the song that birds sing. When I see the morning sunrise or setting sun on the horizon the deep oranges, vibrant corals and splashes of purple I know he is there. His dream of becoming an artist is real. He still is becoming an artist, he paints now a canvas of blue skies with colors so vibrant only God could provide such a color palette! The greatest gift of all…My "Picasso" is learning at the hands of the Master! Once again I am reminded of the renewed promise of Eternal Life.

My Last Journal Entry:

There are many things I have learned in the past three years and seven months, which boils down to 1202 days, which comes down to 28,848 hours or 1,730,880 minutes since my son was ripped out of our family.

One of the first things I have learned is that you have never felt a pain as deep as that of burying your own child, It is not a normal thing to out live your child. It is not normal to watch all of your future go up in smoke nor is it normal to expect to grow old alone without your children by your side.

I have also learned that compassion is not just a word of kindness to another person on the street but it is a feeling that begins in the deepest recesses of my soul. It is the understanding of another's pain and suffering and the need that comes with this compassion to reach out to that aching soul and try as hard as I can to really bring them some comfort during the storm of grief. To reach out and gently help the broken-hearted back up to their feet once again, giving them the strength to make it just one more day.

For I too know just how painful each day has now become and I know how endless the hours are till the end of day when I pray that blessed sleep will find me and bring back to the life I lost. Back to the days when my child played happily at my feet and I knew he was safe as long as I kept him close by my side and held my breathe while asking God endlessly please help to watch over this special blessing you have placed at my feet.

I have learned that tho the days are long and endless they're more tolerable then the dark of night when sleep won't come and I am enveloped in by the lonely painful memories. My mind will not let me go past that last day in the dark of night it only lets me see that painful life since the day My Son was taken Home. Every memory ends with the sound of a shotgun and sirens, the sounds of my own voice screaming NO NOT MY SON!

One thing I have learned is the sound of heart breaking and feel of a shattered heart, it is like I am this big piece of glass that has shattered but some how remains intact. Yet I feel as if someone were to touch me my heart, which is this piece of glass, would shatter into a million pieces at my feet. Yet so many times I have felt that very thing happen just by a familiar smell or sound and as fast as I can pick up those pieces of glass, the faster they fall, each one leaving my heart to bleed.

There is no justice to be found in murder, even if the perpetrator is sentenced he is still alive and my son is still gone. There is no truth in sentencing like in Joshua's case the perpetrator is sentenced to juvenile detention until his 18th birthday, making the sentence 10 months yet he is released after serving only two months, yet my son is not released from his grave.

The perpetrator is free to lead a new life, yet my son has no life and my family no longer exists.

Every single day is a constant struggle, to get through I fill the hours with as much busy work as I can find. Always pushing harder and harder to stay busy so the mind can't wander back in time, so my heart can't feel the empty pain that never seems too dull. With one stupid foolish act of another human being a life is ended and a family forever broken and scarred.

Reckless Horseplay Is Murder

No Excuses!!! If you PLAY like an adult…You should PAY like an adult!

Reckless horseplay is murder. There is an ever-increasing incidence of reckless horseplay. The judicial system is lacking in the knowledge and sensitivity to comprehend the devastation that occurs, when juveniles recklessly and with blatant disregard for human life cause the death of another person IE. Friend.

These incidences of friends killing friends are far too many and are quickly becoming common occurrences. Because the justice system is lacking in compassion and maybe even knowledge, it thinks that as long as a juvenile says I'm sorry I didn't mean it, a simple slap on the wrist is sufficient punishment, never mind the dead child or the dead child's broken family. When will the justice system see that when a juvenile who has been a hunter and has successfully completed a hunters safety course he/she does in fact know exactly what he/she is doing when pointing a gun (loaded or unloaded) at someone?

To point a gun at another individual and continue in the manner chosen even when asked several times by several people to stop pointing the gun and when asked is that gun loaded and responds with "WELL LET'S FIND OUT" pulling the trigger and ending a life is OUT RIGHT MURDER PLAIN & SIMPLE! Record or not he/she needs to be convicted of, at the very least, manslaughter.

All Americans were given the constitutional "RIGHT" to keep and bare arms. Many states now have the "RIGHT" to carry a concealed weapons law. Does that "RIGHT" include the careless mishandling of a firearm? Does that "RIGHT" include the "RIGHT" to allow your child to carelessly play with a loaded weapon, take aim and kill another child? Does that "RIGHT" give you the "RIGHT" to pull a gun and shoot the driver ahead of you because you think he is driving too slow? Does that "RIGHT" allow you or your child to use that firearm to "control the actions" of his/her spouse? Does that "RIGHT" give you or your child the "RIGHT" to use that weapon as means of stopping someone from coming to the aid of your spouse while you are beating her in a public place?

It is not my intention to work towards taking away your right to keep and bare arms but it is my intention to do whatever is possible through this writing and contact with congress to protect your child from the same fate as my child.

It is my intention to hopefully prevent another family from being destroyed by Reckless Horseplay.

Look at your child, see the sparkle in their eyes, look at those radiant smiles see how it light up the world around you, see their future laid out before them. Now go hug them, then go in and make double sure that your "RIGHTS" are safely and securely unloaded and locked up out of harms way, then go make sure that your "Child's RIGHT" is also unloaded and securely locked away, if it is not then just do it. Look at your child and think, really think about what your "RIGHT" can do to your family! If it is not secured properly then do it! If it is your child's firearm and it is nor properly secured then take it away from him/her obviously they are not mature and responsible enough to own one. Take a stand it could be your own child you will save.

Joshua was the greatest gift the Lord has ever bestowed on us. He will forever be sadly missed.

For all those Parents out there, please don't assume that because your child knows that guns are not toys it won't happen to your child. It's the OTHER family who puts our children at risk. Please make sure that the home your child is visiting at does not have weapons UNLOCKED and easily accessible. Please make sure that even though they are teenagers there is a Parent there, who WILL take responsibility for the safety of not just their own child, but ALL THE CHILDREN in their home.

Don't expect the law to take care of it cause that won't happen, my Son is proof of that so are Arkansas's children. So are the tens of thousands of children added to the statistics everywhere, who fill up our cemeteries at an alarming rate.

God Bless our children and our families. God help us all to take responsibility for the world we live in. God help us all to join together and demand that an end to RECKLESS HORSEPLAY be enacted and ENFORCED. Parents are not supposed to bury their children! We are supposed to hold our Grandchildren!

If you agree that reckless horseplay is murder and that we need to start convicting juveniles for these types of crimes then please write your local representatives and senators and demand that they put a stop to RECK-LESS HORSEPLAY. The child you save may be your own!

~Monika, Missouri

I Miss BET'O

January 1998

BET'O—BET'O YOU WERE MY FRIEND
STEVE HAAR REALLY, BUT THE NAME BET'O TOOK YOU
FROM BEGINNING TO END
A BAD ASS ALWAYS, YOU DID YOUR TIME—YOU RACED
THE RACE. A DAMN GOOD PERSON WITH OLD WORLD
VALUES, YET DANGEROUS TO YOURSELF IN SO MANY WAYS.
YOU KNEW YOUR TIME WAS NEAR TO END, GOODBYE'S
WERE NOT YOUR SPECIALTY, BLACK HEARTS YOU COULD
NEVER DEPEND. YOU WILL BE MISSED ALWAYS AND ALBU-
QUERQUE WILL NEVER BE THE SAME. YOU BROUGHT
FRIENDSHIP BACK TO ME AT A TIME THAT I WAS LONELY
AND GOING INSANE. I WILL ALWAYS CHERISH WHAT LIT-
TLE TIME WE HAD, I HOPE THAT WHEREVER YOUR AT
NOW, THE TIME WILL APPRECIATE YOUR GOOD AND NOT
HOLD SO MUCH GREEDY VALUE IN YOUR BAD. I THANK
YOU WITH ALL MY HEART FOR CARING ABOUT ME WHEN
EVERYONE ELSE HAD LEFT ME SO ALONE AND FRIENDS
DIDN'T SEEM TO CARE. ONE YEAR OF LONELY MISSERY
BEFORE YOUR DEATH DID TAKE YOU FROM BEHIND,
THREE MONTHS OF YOUR GOOD HEART MADE ME FEEL
GOOD AGAIN, REALIZING PEOPLE WERE LYING, YOU MADE
ME FEEL UN-SAD. I WISH THINGS COULD HAVE BEEN DIF-
FERENT FOR YOU—THE DEEPNESS OF YOUR DEATH

THOUGH WAS THE DEEPNESS IN YOUR DYING. YOUR
SPIRIT IS ALWAYS WELCOME AROUND ME, YOUR SPIRIT
JUST LIKE WINE. DRINK IT ALL UP TO THE LAST DROP AND
APPRECIATE YOU MY FRIEND I DID. YOU LISTENED TO ME
YOU PROTECTED ME AND SOMEHOW YOU CONNECTED
WITH ME THE WAY I CONNECTED WITH YOU. I WILL
ALWAYS MISS YOU STEVE, YOUR CANDLE ONCE BURNED SO
BRIGHT, THIS TOWN HAS FALLEN APART NOW—GREED
TOOK OVER OUR NIGHTS!

LOVE ALWAYS,
PINK!

PS. Always pink roses, that way you will know it's me—I will always
bring you my pink roses when ever I get the chance or for as long as this
town I stay.

~Laurie Rose Holmes, New Mexico

Ripples in the Pond

November 2000

Somewhere in the town tonight you'll hear a mother cry,
Crying for a daughter murdered by deceit and lies,
A family joined together to weep in shock and grief,
They are tested to the limit in their faith or their belief.

Somewhere in the city there are other families torn,
Grieving for the victim and a son that they have born,
Going back in time to search for some childhood clue,
When were his values lost; they only wish they knew.

A pebble tossed into a pond will ripple far and wide,
Put a name upon each pebble will it be deceit or pride,
Small pebbles, large pebbles all dropped into that pool,
Love, hate, honesty and deceit will finally make the rules.

Somewhere in the town tonight you'll hear the mothers cry,
Think about the pebbles when your mind keeps saying "why"?
Think about those ripples and how far out they reach,
And think about those values that the parents try to teach.

Ripples in the pond that have reached to heaven's door,
When He sent his child and angel to help her spirit soar,
Then he set some things in motion to help ease the pain,
There will be justice in the end for showing Him such disdain.

All around the city people weep for a senseless crime,
Comfort will be another pebble and will take a little time,
Our tears will be raindrops that'll make the ripples break,
And God will be our rock to lean on for salvation's sake.

~ Anonymous, New York

THE HOWLING

March 2000

There is a sound
That if you are very lucky in this life you will never hear,
(and luckier still if you never have a reason to make it)
It's the howling, the howling.

The best actor in the world
Could never recreate it,
For you actually have to feel it-you cannot fake it,
It's the howling, the howling.

I first heard it early one morning this March
My mother on the phone,
Your brother has been murdered,
Oh the howling, the howling.

In the cold morgue, Dad and I had to identify,
His little handicapped body stabbed 36 times, throat slit,
How could someone do this to one so defenseless?
Please God No, oh the howling, the howling.

It came again too soon-that afternoon
I had to tell the children,
Your dear uncle, something terrible, how can I ever explain?
Have you ever heard a child howling, howling?

Seven weeks later, it came again
My in-laws said "we want nothing to do with you now,"
My husband begs them "please, please don't"
How could someone? Oh the howling, the howling.

Christmas now, months later still
On a trip away, my father asleep near me,
In the middle of the night I hear
Again, again-the howling, the howling.

And sometimes I can't help but go
And turn the shower up so high,
Collapse and cry and here it comes
The howling, the howling.

It is the only sound not from your throat,
It only comes from your tormented soul,
My God, pray you never hear
That howling, that howling.

Silence

You don't know what to say or do,
I understand that,
But you must understand that the worst thing,
Is to say or do nothing.

So, here's a tip from someone who's been "on the other side,"
The answer is not hard at all, in fact it's simple,
Look me straight in the eyes, no don't turn away,
Take my hand, hold it tight,
I don't have anything catchy, you won't die by touching me,
And just tell me you care, that's all,
See, it's not so hard,

But the worst thing you can do,
Is to say or do nothing.

And keep on telling me, I need reminding,
You see sometimes the days are dark and the nights are long,
I look forward every day to the mail, to the ringing of the phone,
To someone saying "hello, I'm thinking of you today,"
And bless those people who remember to do this as the months wear on,
But the silence of the days, with no mail, no calls, no contact,
Can be painful,
For the worst thing you can do,
Is to say or do nothing.

No, you just don't "get over" a family member's murder quickly,
Or truly ever I fear,
You don't know how much we rely on you to help us through,
And think of this, perhaps it's a test for you too,
And know that the worst thing you can do,
Is to say or do nothing.

Don't let the months and years go by,
Someday it may be you,
Who needs to hear "I love you and I care,"
But instead you hear only silence,
And you too will finally understand,
That the worst thing you can do,
Is to say or do nothing.

~Kimberly Yazum Jess, New York

OUR ANGELS

July 1999

Savanna and Clifford were killed while visiting their grandmother. They had gone to a cabin owned by their Aunt and had just walked down to the candy store. They along with their 10 year old cousin were about 10 feet up in a private drive when a drunk driver lost control of his car swerved off the side of the road and killed our two children instantly. Our nephew was not physically harmed but will have to forever live with what he saw. My nephew will have to live with what he witnessed that day for the rest of his life. The drunk driver did not let our minds rest for the first year. He played with our emotions for a year before he decided to plead no contest to the charges of murder 3. A year from the day he killed my children the DA called us with this news. He pled no contest on July 12, 2000 and was sentenced on August 21st, 2000 (4 days after their birthday). He was sentenced to 31 1/2 years & 90 days—62 1/2 years & 90 days. He will not be eligible for parole until he serves the minimum sentence of 31 1/2 years & 90 days. This should give the drunk driver plenty of time to think about his action. Remember our children and PLEASE DON'T DRINK AND DRIVE—LOOK AT WHAT IT COST OUR FAMILY!

A Victims Night before Christmas

It's the night before Christmas,
And she sits there alone,
Lost in her memories,
That haunt her once happy home.

No stockings are hung,
By the fireside this year,
Remembering the past,
She wipes away tears.

She thinks to herself,
"I just can't go on."
Nothing much matters,
Now that their gone.

They always loved Christmas,
The lights and the noise,
Especially the children,
When they opened their toys.

"Why" she asks no one,
Again and again,
"Why did this happen?"
"How did it begin?"

She thinks back to July,
That Sunday afternoon,
When this nightmare began,
With absolutely no warning.

She thinks of them walking,
with their cousin,
As their drunk executioner,
Takes his car out of park.

Their walking in a ditch,
They are almost home,
Just children having fun,
Careful and carefree.

Doing everything they have been taught,
Safety was first, looking both ways,
watching out for cars, staying off the road,
So drivers did not have to worry.

His car rounds the corner,
No brake lights come on,
How could he not see them?
In an instant their gone.

They say they felt nothing,
It happened too fast,
How do they know,
What they felt at the last?

These questions and unknowns,
Will never be answered,
The rest of his life,
Their voices will never be heard.

The nightmare continues,
It goes on and on,
The time that it's worst,
Is from dusk to dawn.

She thinks of that person,
That Man! Out with his friends,
She can still be with her family,
Christmas with them all spend.

The anger consumes her,
It eats at her soul,
The long sleepless nights,
Are taking their toll.

She sits there and wonders,
How will she survive?
She wouldn't have to do it,
If that man didn't drink and drive.

She remembers their laughter,
She feels so alone,
Not that it matters,
Their not coming home.

"Their not coming home,"
Words that cut like a knife,
Their sentence was death,
Hers is for life.

They were her children,
The light of her life,
She screams at the darkness,
"I want this nightmare to end!"

~Donna M. Scheck, North Carolina

GYPSY'S ANGELS

April 1999

Heather Lynne Williamson, who was suddenly taken from me through DOMESTIC VIOLENCE by her 18 mo. old baby's father.

Heather was stalked and hurt on April 15,1999,when he broke her left wrist that day.

He threaten to kill her, and her baby son. Heather, lived in Puerto Rico, with her baby. Heather, was on the run for her life, the last two weeks of her life.

She went to work, and hid with co-workers, her special friends those last few days of her life.

Heather had 12 protective orders (P.O.) against this man. To me, P.O. are only pieces of paper, if the officials do not enforce them. Laws have to be changed here, and over there, and abroad, as too many of our children are being murdered!

Heather, was told by an police officer that he was in jail on a $40,0000 bail, so my daughter thought that she was safe to go alone into her apartment. But she was not, as he had been hiding in her apartment after he broke into it days earlier, just waiting to kill her.

Heather was so sweet, kind, caring, and very innocent-as in her heart, she saw good in this person, not the evil. She kept telling her co-workers/friends-"He, won't kill me, because I am the Mother of his child." But my darling Heather, was so wrong because he did kill her.

Heather left her baby with his aunt for the last couple days of her life as she was actually running for her life. By doing this kind, loving act, she saved her baby from being killed also.

If the baby would have been with her, there is no doubt that I would have buried two instead of one.

Heather, had just found a cute home, that she was planing on moving into on the other side of the island that same day that she was murdered.

She went into her apartment for her rent money that she had hid there. We think that she heard a noise in her bedroom, so she went to check it out. That is when he jumped out at her, blocking her between the dresser, crib, and bed. He had hid in her bedroom closet waiting for her. He attacked her from behind, he argued with her, and beat Heather until she went unconscious. He cut her throat, and stabbed her many numerous times. We are not sure of the exact knife wounds, more than 20. It could have been 150, 350, 550 or more times but she died from internal major trauma as all her major organs were destroyed.

I was devastated to hear of the loss of my darling, daughter Heather. And if that was not enough pain to bear, my grandson was taken into protective custody hours after the murder.

We, my mom and I; were not able to talk to him, nor see him while we were on the island.

Heather, left no will so my darling grandson's fate now falls into the hands of the officials and they are very slow in moving paper work, and justice!

He recently cut a deal with the DA office for the murder charge. He got second degree murder instead of first degree murder. He got only 35 years in prison instead of 125 years.

Where is justice for the cold, ugly, senseless act of murder towards a young women who only 22 yrs. old with her whole life ahead of her with her two beautiful sons?

Heather, left a four year old son with his Dad and grandparents back here in the states, and an innocent baby in Puerto Rico, who has been moved 3 times since his "Mommy, was murdered." "Where is justice? and safety for this precious baby ", I ask you?

Where is justice, for that monster taking my only daughter away from me, who was also, my best friend, that I miss dearly, every second minute hour of the day, and night

I worry about my grandson's, health and safety, so I promised my daughter, when I kissed her good-bye, that I will do everything possible to bring my grandson back to the states, with me, where she wanted him to be. That was a request that she asked of one of her friends just 24 hours before her death.

You have read my daughter Heather's story about her murder, and you are probably wondering why she did not flee to the states, back home. The answer, is because the states, were no longer her home. Her home became Puerto Rico, where she lived with her baby.

Heather, worked as a waitress in a nearby town in a restaurant in a large, fancy tourist hotel. She loved her job, and liked/loved her co-work-ers a lot. They became her family there. These wonderful people were a Godsend to me immediately after the murder. They helped me, with talking to the police, social services, morgue, and the crematory as I do not speak, nor understand any Spanish, at all.

Losing a child to murder is very heartbreaking, and a very trauma shock to a person. My life has been altered forever from the murder of my beautiful daughter Heather A lot of cruel remarks were spoken after her death, but what I can say to those remarks is this "Do not condemn some-one-unless you walk in their shoes!!!"

Heather, was smart, gentle, kind, caring, loving, funny, my daughter, and my Best Friend. She never told me, about the abuse. I knew of two former incidents when I tried to talk her into coming back to the states, but she loved the island, and did not want to leave there.

Heather was young, 22, she did not have experiences of the world, nor did she personally know of evil. She never saw the evil of this Man, but we all did. People argued with her to tell me the truth about her situation, but she did not want to worry me. They told her to run, before she was murdered. She would not, because she saw only good in this Man. She really thought in her heart, that because she had his baby, that he would not kill her.

She was in denial, from his constant stalking, beatings, and threatening of her. She must have felt trapped, like she had no where to go. If only she would have told us, then we could have helped her, and saved her life.

Heather was so innocent. Heather was murdered nine months after the relationship ended.

This is usually the most dangerous time for an abused person. As in most situations, this is when victims of abuse are murdered. If you know of a relative, or close friend, show them this story, and I plead with you, tell them to grab their baby, or children, and run as fast as they can.

An abusive relationship does not go away, unless you, as the victim take the control away from the abuser, and take control for your own life.

Why! am I a survivor of domestic violence? Because I took control of my own life back.

Also I turned my life over to the Lord, and asked for his help. I turned state's evidence against my ex-husband, and I put him away. I relocated out of state. Actually Heather and I ran for years state to state, until I thought that it was safe to stop. I raised Heather, practically on my own, for several years. I was remarried, but he was so jealous, so I divorced again. Heather was a good child, she was excellent student in school, she was very gifted in singing, playing all types of musical instruments, chorus at school, softball, and cheerleader.

She was gentle, kind, loving, with a sense of humor. She did not deserve to be taken from us so violently. She had so much to live for.

No mother should have to bury her child, or children. It is so wrong.

ANGER

Anger, I feel so much inner rage as to what has happened to you.
A person, mother, daughter, victim of Domestic Violence.

Anger, at the pain you suffered before your death.
Anger at your murderer for his cold, evil torture he bestowed upon you, my beloved child.

Anger at the government, judges, police, murderer, his family members who knew of his threats and terrorizing of you, and silently stood by and let the violence continue until your murder.

Anger of the senseless act of the beating, murder and mutilation of your beautiful face and body.

Anger at your neighbors who heard your screams and pleas for help but did nothing to help you!

Anger at these same people for not helping you but they had their nerve to give their personal statements to the police and to the crew and local papers.
Statements about your life, and your cries for help before your murder!
Anger at the police and the government for not protecting you from being murdered.

Anger at police, FBI and rest of government for not locating a mother that her daughter was just murdered. I had to find this out 24 hours later by one of your co-workers who was devastated by your death and the fact that a mother in the states had no clue her daughter passed away, called me a day later to inform me of your death.

Anger of your baby taken by police force and thrown into an orphanage for 3 ½ weeks after your murder. Anger at not being allowed to see my grandson after his mother's death, my daughter.

Anger after grandma and I landed in this country where we sat in a police station for over six hours waiting, waiting for nothing! Anger at the social worker who took our statements in confidentiality and then broke it. Anger at his families lies about me, you.

Anger that no one would take me immediately to you!

Anger that you laid unclaimed for four days in a cold morgue.
Anger that I was only allowed to view your lips to your hair.
Anger at your beaten face, every square inch by that mad man!

Anger of your wounds!
Anger of your pain and suffering!
Anger that no one helped to save your life!

Anger that I was not permitted to view your whole body and to hold your beautiful hands for the last time. Anger that some monster could hurt my child, my daughter, my baby, torn at my heart and soul.

Anger at the lies. Anger at the injustice so far that has been done to you. Anger at the injustice to the baby.

Anger at the pain and suffering that has fallen on your oldest son here in the states.
Anger seeing this precious child's pain in his eyes.
Anger that he had to lose his Mommy at such an early age.

Anger: we as victims have no rights!

~ Linda S. Morton, Pennsylvania

ABANDONED AGAIN

March 1980, April 2000

We are born into this world as innocent human beings. We are loved and cherished by our parents. As children we adore our parents, longing for their love, trust and stability. We seek safety in our parents; we seek their guidance and love.

Even when we are born into families that are less than perfect we still value our parents' love. I loved my parents. I adored my father and admired my mother. I never wanted anything more than my parents' love.

My father was a pillar of strength to me. A tall, handsome and strong man that showed compassion for the world. He helped others, spent time with family and shared his life with me. We would hike, fish, hunt, fly kites and talk. I could talk to my father about anything and everything. I remember the first time I heard a curse word on the school bus I asked my father what it meant and he explained the word to me. He taught me how to do construction; I would go on job estimates with him and even go up on the roofs of homes he was working on. He always had time for me; he was always there for me. I was and still am Daddy's girl.

I remember the day, a chilly March Sunday that we spent loading firewood, singing, dancing and talking. I remember him lying on the floor listening to music. I remember him smiling at me and I thought how lucky I was to have a Dad to love and protect me. But that chilly day turned into a day that I can never forget.

In a turn of events that I can't even begin to explain, violence erupted. I had seen the violence before but it would always end the same. Not this time. During the heat of a battle a gun was picked up, fought over and fired. I can still hear the gun shot ringing. I stood there looking between the wood slat wall at the top of the stairs and watched my father stagger and fall. My pillar of strength fell like the trees we had cut down.

I moved to look at him, not knowing what to do. I wanted to go to him but at that moment fear took over my body. What do I do? I could hear him breathing; it was a different type of breathing, and something I never heard before.

I remember trying to call the operator and couldn't remember who I was or where I lived. I left the phone hanging while I went back to look at my father. I still didn't know what to do. I heard my father, he repeated over and over "Traci, I love you, remember I always love you."

The remainder of the night was a whirlwind of events between the ambulance, neighbors, relatives, police, Pastor and everyone talking. But no one seemed to know what I saw. I couldn't tell them, they couldn't know. My father was gone, my life was gone, and my safety was gone. That night I sat alone on my bed, a twelve-year-old girl alone and lost. I felt completely abandoned by the person that I loved most in the world.

I still hear my father telling me he loved me and I haven't forgotten him. There is still a part of me that is the lonely twelve-year-old girl who wants to go sit on her bed. There is a large part of me that is still my father. I miss him more than anyone could ever imagine. I wanted him to be here during my life, I expected him to be here for me but he's gone.

I think of the times when he taught me how to drive the riding lawn mower and then would play kickball with me. I remember how devastated I was the first time I shot a rabbit and how proud my father was of me hunting with him. I remember when I smashed my bike and he had to take me to the dentist. I remember on Friday nights we would go to town to the bank and visit an aunt and uncle. I remember so many good times and how much he loved me.

I also know how lonely I have been for so long. Wanting my father's love, wanting him here to protect me. I remember how schoolmates didn't know what to say to me. I remember how everyone thought it would get better. I had told myself that he went on a hunting trip and would come back one day. But he never came back. The day he was buried (after cremation), it rained, and I remember thinking how could a big strong man be in a small container. My childhood was buried on that rainy day.

My father was 32 years old when he died. When I turned 32 I couldn't imagine my life being over. I kept thinking I have so much to live for, my life is just beginning. I couldn't imagine my daughters growing up without me. It was the point in my life that I finally started to deal with my father's death. It took almost twenty years for me to finally accept his death; to come to terms with myself on what I saw that day. I started therapy and hoped to move on in my life and move past part of the depression.

During this time I confronted some of my other losses. My mother and I always had a rocky relationship. I never wanted anything more in my life than my mother's love. My father always seemed giving and my mother was hard to please. I felt emotionally abandoned by my mother. I never felt her love, never felt the bond I should have had, never felt what I wanted during my life.

My mother and I went in waves. For three years we got along and for three years we wouldn't speak. Our problems were always trivial but we never seemed to connect. All I ever wanted was for her to love me. I adored and admired all she had accomplished in her life. I wanted her to love me for who I was. I could never be myself around her because she said my personality was too much like my father's. The pain was so strong between us that we couldn't move past it. I always had hope; I always had the dream that one day we would be close.

In March of 2000 I asked my sister if I wanted mom's number would she give it to me. She said she would. I told her I wasn't ready to call yet; I needed some more time. I was so fearful of being rejected and yet all I wanted was my mom.

Yet twenty years, one month, sixteen days and some three hours after my father's death, my mother was dead. I never got to call her. I never got to tell her that I loved her. I was 32 years old and my mother was dead. I was an orphan and abandoned again.

The night my mother's murder happened, I was on the phone with a friend. While we were talking I kept telling my friend something bad was happening, I could feel it in my soul. Then a car accident happened outside my house. I thought the accident was the bad thing. I couldn't sleep. I had finally gone to bed and little did I know a half-hour later my phone started to ring. I couldn't hear the phone and finally my daughter came to get me. I thought for sure that the call was about a friend who recently had surgery for cancer. It was my sister.

"Mom's dead, he killed mom and then he killed himself!"

I couldn't believe the words. All I could do was scream. How could the person I wanted my entire life, the woman who brought me into this world be gone? I couldn't believe twenty years later that my mother was dead, dead at someone else's hand.

I hadn't seen my mother for three years. She had married and moved. The man she married is the same man that killed her. I will never forget feeling like a stranger, like I was looking in on my own life in disbelief.

I cried and searched for the people closest to me. I received calls from people I hadn't heard from in years. We planned her memorial service, she had wanted to be cremated and from the head trauma she would have to be cremated. Her husband, my stepfather, had bludgeoned her to death with a hammer. She was sitting and watching TV and he smashed her skull, not once, not twice but three times. I am told the first blow killed her instantly. He confessed his crime and then shot himself in the head.

I saw her house and where it happened. The house had been cleaned but the blood had soaked through the carpet to the floorboards. I saw her blood on the walls. I moved a curtain and saw her remains clinging to the glass. I saw the bullet hole from where the bullet had passed through his skull and went into a cabinet. I saw his blood. I could see what had happened by the pattern of the blood splatters on the walls and ceiling. A child should never see a parent's blood on the wall and this is what I last saw of my mother.

I have been searching my mind and heart for the good memories of my mother and I. The memories are harder to find than those with my father. I feel as if all my hopes and dreams were shattered on April 18, 2000. I never realized how much I had wanted her love until her death. I always knew I wanted to be with her but always feared being pushed away. Before I had a 50/50 chance of having a mother/daughter relationship with her, now there is nothing, zilch, it's all gone.

I always feel as if God blessed me with three daughters to compensate what I lacked in a relationship with my own mother. I still want to be the daughter having her mother's unconditional love. I grieve my father, my mother and what I will never have. I grieve not having a "normal" child-hood. I grieve not having parents.

I resent the fact that my children are growing up without grandparents. I resent that they have been cheated of a whole family. My children are young and innocent and yet they have already lost both their grandparents. Violence has already been a part of their lives.

I resent the fact that there are too many people who complain about their parents. Too many people disrespect what they have been blessed with in life. I don't have the option to complain because I don't have parents. I envy my friends, their families and parents.

I resent the fact that I have devoted too much time on loss. I resent what I don't have and have become incapable of having.

I keep thinking what are the chances of losing one parent to violence let alone both? I wonder what evil lurks out there in the world? I have gone through more stages and emotions than I thought humanly possible. I have spent weeks of not wanting to leave my own home. I keep thinking of what life could have been and what it will be. You can't help but think of the would've, could've and should've.

I have learned a lot since the death of my parents. There is a stigma attached to murder. People seem to think they might catch "murder" if they are with you. People will treat you in a demeaning manner without even realizing what their own actions convey. They comment on what was wrong, what would provoke an event and don't take the time to look at the complete picture. People don't take the time to comprehend the pain that surrounds all the people who are left here to cope with the loss.

Unless you have experienced this loss you can't understand that this loss is a part of you. Just as an infant born into this world is a part of their parents, as an adult my parents' murders are a part of who I am today. I have learned two valuable lessons. One if you have something to say then say it. I will always have to live with the fact that I didn't call my mother. Two enjoy each day to the fullest with no regrets because you never know what tomorrow holds. In a moment your life can be forever changed.

After my father's death, I never wanted to love, I feared anyone leaving. I feared closeness and trusted no one. I fear abandonment. With my mother's death these emotions have been reinforced. At times I fear people, fear the unknown, fear my instincts. My heart is filled with three large voids, my father, my mother and the love that has been lost. I fear ever being abandoned again.

When your life is filled with trauma and negative experiences you don't know how to enjoy the positive. In many aspects I feel that I am trying to live again. I have lost so much, a part of my spirit has been dying inside while the positive part of me attempts to emerge. There are times I can't tell the difference between the positive and negative. I tend to sabotage all that is good in my life because I carry fear and try to have control over my life experiences. This destructive and impulsive behavior is my self-defenses working in high gear. I have so much to give and share but my fear of loss and abandonment make it difficult for me to share.

Every move and chance I take, I take my past into factor. The loneliness can be unbearable. I have found safety in my own world yet thrive for a life filled with positive emotional companionship. The emotions tend to fly faster than I can feel, perhaps that is why it is so easy to become numb. I have lived a majority of my life numb for then the pain doesn't hurt as much. Now that I am learning to live again, I am learning to feel and let go of some of the pain and anger that has numbed me. I am learning to let go of the part of my spirit that has been dying inside so the positive part of me can come back to life. I don't want to be numb anymore, I don't want to feel abandoned anymore. All of these processes sound simple but are more complex than we can imagine.

I will always miss my father. I miss so much of the good, I miss what I had and how much I love him. I miss knowing that he was there, security and his love. With my mother, just because we weren't close doesn't mean I don't feel. In some ways her death is harder because I never received the love I deserved, I never had the security I desired and all my dreams have been shattered. I never took the time to tell her how beautiful she was, how much I admired her strength and how much I love her. No matter if you are close or not with a loved one, the violent death is still hard. There is no closure, no answers and no chance for good-byes.

Each day I pray for understanding, peace and for my parents to know that I love them. I pray that no one else can feel the deep pain that I feel. I feel as if I have been repeatedly abandoned in my life. There are days when I don't know how I will make it through. That is when I turn to my safe people, my safe friends who listen and help guide me through the pain. I pray for the strength to accept everything that has happened in my life. If you can just imagine a valuable part of your spirit that has been taken away and then try to live, your life is not the same.

~Traci Bieber Nelson, Pennsylvania

My Memories of Carl and Valda

August 1990

DAD

Dad's values and lessons:

Honesty

Work as hard as you can

Keep your word at all times and if you can't make sure to let the person you were making the promise to know

Accomplish as much as you can without hurting anyone on the way

Treat everyone the same

Remember the struggles of the less fortunate, both financially and physically

Remember your manners at all times, even the hard times

Enjoy nature, and use the simple things to relax you.

My memories of him:

Long, long talks in the back yard, about most everything

Long discussions about what was in today's newspaper

Riding the train at the zoo (always the 1st stop), always remembering to scream when going through the dark tunnel

Going for long rides in the cool beauty of the evenings, always an "ice cream stop" on the way, gliding on the road with sweetness in your mouth at the same time

The smell of pancakes and bacon on Sunday mornings, listening to the top 40 on the radio while everything was cooking, the taste of bacon with pancake syrup

The smell of pinto beans, ham and cornbread cooking on a Saturday afternoon, while I was safe in my room, list in the world of my books and records

Driving all over town on a cold, clear winter night to find the right Douglas Fir Christmas tree

Watching movies together in my first apartment after eating hamburger steaks with fried potatoes

Coming to help me with flat tires in the middle of rush hour traffic

Eating handfuls of the Christmas cookies I spent hour baking

His despair at not being able to understand Mom.

GRANDMA

Memories:

Getting to stay overnight at her place, the next day always getting to see a movie and go out to lunch at Burger King

Trips at Christmas to the graves of her husband (my grandfather) and son (my uncle), with bright, foil-wrapped poinsettias to leave after saying a prayer for them and the rest of the family still alive

Dinners at Luby's cafeteria, where she'd put bites of what she was having on my plate, and smile while doing it

Going to the Nutcracker ballet every Christmas: the feel of her small arm in mine as we navigated the steps, the smell of our fancy makeup and new special dresses; how she'd start telling me stories from her life long ago while we waited for the ballet to begin; how she'd jab my side with her arm when the mice and the Rat King came onstage; the time we got lost on the way home and ended up laughing about it for years afterward

Going to see the Everly Brother, where she said some of their songs were "too fast and too loud."

~Laura, Texas

Silence Kills

March, 1995

Nicole was only 7, when on her Dad's birthday, in March 1995, she was taken by a neighbor, raped repeatedly and murdered. After three days of searching, an entire community all in force, she was found by police, in a neighbor's attic, only a block from where she was taken. This 34 year Old man, had always had a strong "desire to have sex with a little girl"…(this is what he said). I just call him the Animal. There, in my opinion, are no other descriptions to fit him. He sits on Texas death row; I'm sure getting fat, watching TV, and working crossword puzzles. This man is so cold, that after he murdered her on Thursday night, her went to work on Friday, and even discussed the "missing little girl" with co-workers. Took his lunch, and ever so kindly offered to share it with a co-worker who had none. What a good guy he is.

These are some of the facts. The gory details don't make it more interesting just gives him more attention.

I always felt, from the moment I heard she was missing, I want just one more hug. So the dream I had about 6 months after her death was not surprising to me, but so very real. I was standing in front of her little white coffin, looking down at her precious little face, and telling her to set up…Set up…Grandma needs just one more hug…and I felt I was willing her to set up…and all of a sudden she did, and smiled at me and reached out her arms…I tried to reach for her to give her that hug, but I was froze and I couldn't get to her. I woke up, in tears. I know that dream was a gift from God, showing me that it was not my time to be with Nicole, she was

110

home with him now. It also reminded me that, the Animal took her away from us, physically, but he can not take her spirit away from us.

The thing that has been taken, that could be repaired, is our family communication about Nicole. I mention her, and you can almost feel the gasps. Her name brings such horror and that just breaks my heart. She lived, and we are allowing that Animal to take her memory away. It has been five years, no ones pain is any greater than anyone else's. But because so many feel it too painful to discuss, a precious little girl that touched so many lives, is put in a closet. It almost makes me feel they are putting her back in that attic. Are they attaching some sort of shame to Her? I'm sorry, I just don't understand.

Someone, please talk to me about my little girl.

In loving memory of my Sweet Nicole.

Dear Nicole
12/15/1995
Dear Nicole,

Christmas is just a few days away and you know how I miss you. The holidays will always be the most painful times. I have your brother and sisters and your cousins, but that won't fill the empty place in my heart for you.

You gave so much love to us all. Your hugs and kisses can't be forgotten. The selfish part of my heart lets the tears flow down my face, because I want you back. Grandmothers are not supposed to be left here standing over their Granddaughter's grave.

You know how much you were loved and I know that for sure. That knowledge helps. But when you see me with tears flowing, you know I'm missing you; I'm loving you; trying to touch you, to remember how your hair felt, to remember how your little arms felt around my neck. Trying to feel you setting in my lap with your arm around my shoulder. I want to see your sparkling blue eyes smiling up at me. I want to feel that energy you had for life. I want to touch that sweet soft skin on your cheek, and I want to see you twirl around in another fancy dress.

My baby Nicole, you left your mark on this earth. No one, who loved you, will ever be quite the same without you. The sad feeling we have, missing you, is our selfishness. We wanted our world to stay the same, with you here with us. We wanted to go on, without seeing that all the people we love are mortal and can, at God's will be taken to his kingdom. It hurts my darling that a messenger from the devil took you away. It bothers me that your last sight on this earth was not someone who loved you, and you died with fear in your eyes. All we can do is promise you that everything possible will be done to make sure you didn't die in vein. Because of you, that devil's messenger will be taken away from any chance to harm another beautiful little girl like you.

With all my love always,

Grandma Linda

This is dedicated to the Asst. DA, who tried this case and Won! You will always have our gratitude.

~Grandma Linda, Texas

Not Even Death Will Keep us Apart

July 1997

It haunts me in the night,
I awake as the tears begin to fall.
You put up such a fight,
As you were dragged down the hall.

I can't believe the things they did to you,
Half of them didn't know you at all.
I couldn't believe it was true,
Even after I got the phone call.

The gruesome details I couldn't bear to hear,
I found myself gasping for breath.
I could feel that you were near,
Nothing could stop our friendship, not even death.

Did you live your life in every way?
Did you ever regret even a single day?
Could you possibly miss me more than I miss you?
Could I have saved you if I only knew?

I can still hear your voice in my mind,
I see your face in my dreams.
Some night I dream of the fun times,
Other nights I can hear your screams.

You were one of my greatest gifts,
I never got to tell you that.
I didn't get to tell you a lot of things.
But I know you will forgive me for that.

You now lay alone never to breathe again,
I look upon your face and wonder.
I now know you were angel sent from heaven,
I know you are here every time I hear the thunder.

Ashes to ashes, dust to dust,
A prayer for the deceased.
I will cry if I must,
But you must rest in peace.

~Lisa Barron, Washington

GIFT OF LOVE

August 1993

The time goes fast, but the hours go slow,
To any question of hope, the answers "no"
To think that a phone's innocent ring
Would change your life with the news' it brings.
"Oh God, Oh no, this just can't be,
I can't get this straight, what are you telling me?"
There is no time now to debate
"How bad, where's he at, who could possibly hate...?
Him enough to take his life at their own will
"calm down," they say, "Please take this pill"
The ride, the hopes, the dread, the pain
"Will he be o.k.?", then you pray in vain
You arrive at the ER, see the guard and say
"Where's he at, my son?" He says come this way
You are taken to a room, a special place
There's a phone, tissues, your private space
And you realize from memory as it comes to you,
This courtesy is extended when little hope's in view
And you beg "Not here, I'll sit with the rest."
"But Maam," he replies "I think this is best."
So the inevitable now is only minutes away,
You see your son, and you hear them say
"I am so sorry, there is really nothing we can do"

and you see for yourself what they are saying is true
Calls are made to his preacher, family and friends
"Do you want to see him once more before his life ends?"
A crowd is around, yet you feel so alone
The grief shared by all on their face is shown
It is over now, except the wait
To guarantee a machine can't change his fate.
So now, many reluctantly begin to leave
This is so unreal, so hard to believe.
The time is here to decide what to do,
He's gone, now it's totally up to you
Should I let this pass and simply go
With this need for organs, the answers "No"
If in his death, one life he could save
Before they lay his body, in its grave,
I know my son, He would want to give
A part of himself to help others live.
I know his heart, I know what he would do
I have heard him sing "I would die 4 U"
I asked since then from God above
That my son's O.K., this boy I love...
I received it too, and to this day
I know he's with God, he is O.K.
His body was only his earthly shell
A place for this heart and soul to dwell
I have no regrets, I have learned to much
Just how many lives his gift did touch
I'm not sorry at all, not to this day
No better tribute to my son could be paid
That someone else sees love through his eyes too...
And, Brad, another lives longer because of you
God didn't want his body, he had his soul

To be buried forever in a deep, dark hole
When through his wisdom, this knowledge is known
And that through his senseless death, his love for man could be shown.

A TRIBUTE TO MY SON, BRAD WILKERSON

~Linda Wilkerson Wolford, West Virginia

My Mother and My Brother were Both Murdered

October 1999

Bill goes to the door
In the middle of the night.
Then runs, falls, dies,
A nightmarish sight.

Mother is inside.
She sees her son die.
She dies as she thinks-
Why Oh God! Why?

They're sleeping and warm
Safe in bed,
Then screaming, dying,
Quiet again, both dead.

Evil slithered out
From under a rock.
Then slithered back again
After firing the shots.

Before, life is normal;
My world is secure.
After, life is twisted,
Agony to endure.

Before, I have family;
They've always been there.
After, is weeping,
And utter despair.

Two honest people,
Loving and kind.
A Mother and Brother,
Proud they are mine.

Two lives, two deaths,
My Mother, my Brother
Two caskets, two graves,
One by the other.

I stand and stare
At brown caskets and leaves.
Leaves falling and spinning
From gold-colored trees.

I must be dreaming;
I shake my head.
This can't be real.
They couldn't be dead.

One minute life is normal,
As life should be.
Then the telephone rings.
The call is for me.

One minute it's fall,
A cool, rainy day.
Then the rains on the inside
And won't go away.

Written on the anniversary of the murders of her mother Evelyn and her brother Bill Leis, October 8, 2000.

~Mary, Wisconsin

How I Feel

January 1998

On January 12, 1998 I lost my only sister, Laurie Lees (nee Grealy). Laurie was murdered by her husband of almost 10 years while her daughter (age 4) and son (age 2) slept in the adjoining rooms.

At the time I wrote this, my family and I were not only grieving the loss of Laurie, but we were also having to deal with police, lawyers, the courts, child advocates, child supervisors, the murders family and the murderer himself since he was allowed out on bail pending trial.

I felt like I couldn't trust anyone and that nobody cared or wanted to help us. I'm happy to say that some of those feelings have changed as of today, September 14, 2000 the children are safely in our families custody and the murderer is in jail for life, minimum 10 years. Now we can remember Lore and celebrate what was her life with her children.

My goal with this piece was two fold; 1. To simply vent, and it helped and 2. Try and educate society as to what survivors of homicide go through. I recommend you have someone read this piece to you while you as it says sit down, close your eyes and listen.

Thank You

How I Feel

How am I? You query.
Do you really, truly want to know? I wonder.
What's up?…You wonder.
Are you capable of understanding…I think.
How am I feeling?…You ask.

Please, sit down, close your eyes and listen with your heart and soul…and I will tell you.

You are at home, sitting in your favorite chair, in your favorite room…
You are happy, relaxed, feeling confident in yourself & your direction in life.
You are at peace with the world and yourself.

You slowly open your eyes…
You are happy to see your entire family sitting in the room with you.
As you eyes focus you realize everyone is tied to their seats…as are YOU!

A hooded figure slowly enters the room.
All you can see is its mouth…
The figure walks over to you bound family…and KILLS your sister.
Grins, cackles and says, "oops, I didn't mean to do that."

In horror you try to break free…but can't.
You want to help her, save her…but can't.
All you can do is sit, sobbing and sobbing to the point of vomiting.

You now sit, exhausted and in complete disbelief…
Your blood slowly begins to boil.

The figure turns and plunges a shovel deep into your stomach!
Then slooowly, pulls it out…leaving a painful gapping void in your soul.

You now lie on the floor in a pool of sorrow,
Trying to hold yourself together, mentally and physically...
Your blood continues to boil.

Now you hear sobbing and screams!
You look up to see the figure cutting, burning, maiming your family...
All the while it smiles, cackles and taunts you.

Again, in horror you try to help them.
Try to break free...but can't.
You have to help yourself before you can help the...but

Their Screams!
Their Cries!
Their Anger!

They try to fight off the figure...but can't.
Then you and your family,
Together,
Try to protect your now dead sister's two small children...
You succeed...for now.

The hooded figure stops, laughs and removes one of its many masks...
It is your dead sister's husband!
So called loving Father of the two children you & your family are protecting.

Yet again...you sit in disbelief,
So many thoughts race inside your mind,
That you can't think...your blood boils more, and more.

Two more hooded figures enter the room.
The first proclaims the children must visit their father,
For "we must" consider the "rights" of the accused.

This figure removes it's hood to reveal a multi-headed monster.
Heads of every judge, lawyer and police officer you've ever seen.
Heads of child advocates, child supervisors, the killers three brother and ironically,
One sister.
Everyone one of them…. Blind.
This figure is, "the system".

The second figure starts pouring salt and acid all over you and your family.
Forcing you to move away from the children.
The figure grabs the children and calls you and your family evil!
Then leaves with her nose in the air.

You lie there with your family…

Lost…
Alone…
Confused…

Most of all, everyone is now a completely changed individual.
All thinking thoughts of you would never have believed could be imagined
By anyone…Let alone, by you.

Frustration…Anger…
Loss…Anger…
Fear…Anger…

The overwhelming desire to harm or kill.
To do to him, what he did to your sister, to You, your Family.
Her Friends and Relatives, Neighbors, Co-Workers,
The Lady at her corner store and so on and so on…

But most of all,
To those two loving innocent children,
Who loved their Mommy more than anything in the world.

May I ask you now…
How are you feeling? But wait.
Before you answer, please…feel that feeling…live that feeling.

Now, multiply it by a billion billions!
Zap it with one million volts!
Drop it off the CN Tower into a pool of glue!
Kick it through the alleys of New York!
Now, take it back into the center of your soul.

So…*How are you feeling?*

That feeling, is equal to 1% of

HOW I FEEL…

~Ryan Grealy, Canada

My Dear Sisters Murder

2000

I am writing this from what feels a selfish perspective because I am writing about my pain and my life before and after my sister's horrific murder. This is partly because we know very little about what happened to my sister and because I can't ask her how she is now.

My sister, Khia (not her real name), was murdered in an Asian country with a different language, alphabet and political system. In our search for information about her murder we have encountered translation difficulties, blocks due to international relations, the agendas of governments, incompetence by all the authorities involved in Europe (where I live), and a media ban on her murder in the country where she was murdered. This is no exception; reporting any unsolved criminal case is banned in this country. I suspect that these other problems are not exceptional in cases of overseas murder either. Nevertheless we have been told that the local police are trying as hard as they can. We have been told if we complain or go to the media, the local police will react and stop helping us. The authorities in the country of her murder have offered their condolences. We have been told by the authorities in Europe that this same system does not care what we do raising the media profile of the case will have no positive effect. Given the human rights abuses in the country where my sister was murdered, maybe this is true. It is seven months since her murder and we are feeling depleted.

This search is for information about what happened to my best friend, my perfect older sister, and the person who had been there for me for as long as I have existed. We had planned to bring up our children together, we confided in one another, we bought the same clothes, and we shared friends and good times as well as bad.

Khia was stabbed at least 30 times in broad daylight in a busy place. She had been wanting to travel for a long time and had saved hard for her trip around the world. The country where she was murdered was her last destination on her long trip. Khia had many other injuries but due to post mortems in different continents by pathologists who do not communicate, we still do not know how she received all her other injuries. I am left with trying to imagine what could have occurred.

Seven months ago I got one of my last emails from Khia, she said "Look after yourself emotionally! Big sister instructions!!" It made me smile at the time and brought tears to my eyes when I read it. I had just left a job I hated, I had a new boyfriend, and I was doing very well in my new work: I was happy. Usually on a Saturday night I had at least three options of which group of friends to see. I really missed my sister but we emailed regularly and still had our sisterly chats and confidences. I telephoned her once while she was away and cried through the call because I missed her so much and it was so good to hear her voice again. I decided I did not care how much the call cost and we talked for half an hour, I am so pleased I did, as I will never speak to her again. My life was good, I was busy enjoying the city I had recently moved to and enjoying being me. Khia had told me how much she was dreading resuming normal life and coming back to cold Europe. I suggested that if she liked it out there so much why didn't she live there? I wanted her to be happy most of all. She told me, she did not want to stay in Asia, and she wanted to come home at the end of her trip.

Three days before Khia's murder I went out with friends for a celebration. Now when I look back at this, it seems strange how normal life was and that I could be out having fun when my sister was about to die. I have to remind myself she was still alive at this time. I proudly told my friends about my older sisters and her travels. I would emphasize to my new boyfriend how close I was to Khia, how we used to speak on the 'phone every day. Unfortunately he never had the chance to meet her. I had an interview for my dream job in a few days time; I was trying to get a job where I could write.

Khia and I agreed that I would sell my car and drive her car while she was away. She warned me, "you better sell it quickly, I am coming back soon, I am back in six weeks!" That news to me was like rain at the end of a long drought.

It was about 7.30 am, I was sitting in the lounge eating my breakfast in my pajamas when I heard my mobile 'phone ringing. My new work involved early morning calls about where I needed to work each day. As I already knew the arrangements for that day and not being a morning person I left the 'phone to ring. My main 'phone rang, then my mobile started ringing again after my land line had clicked onto the answerphone. I was thinking, "Someone really wants to talk to me" and going upstairs to answer the 'phone. It was my mother, she said, "I have some bad news." "Yes," I replied, we had been expecting my father to die for several years and I was half expecting to hear that he had. "It is very bad news" she stressed. I thought, "Get on with it!" My mother has a habit of taking a long time to get to the point and I was getting annoyed. "Khia is dead," she said. My world fell apart.

I can not remember what I said after that but I know I started crying straight away. I told her I would come home with my younger sister and my boyfriend would drive us. I had thought these things through already because of my father's long illness; I had been preparing for his death for years but never my sisters. I knew no one is immortal but I just thought she would continue to always be there.

It took about an hour and half to get through to my younger sister as she is such a heavy sleeper, she kept sleeping through the 'phone ringing. She woke up to numerous messages saying, "don't go to work", "call home, it is really bad news", "DON'T go to work". She too thought my father had died or otherwise that someone had had a non-fatal car accident.

It took about an hour for my boyfriend to come to me. I remember walking around the house crying in complete shock knowing I need to find someone desperately. I found my housemate in the kitchen and told her my sister had died. She hugged me for ages while I sobbed convulsively; I needed that hug so much. She told me she had sisters too and did not know what she would do if one of them died. The phone rang and it was my younger sister, I arranged to go over to her home later. Somehow I managed to wash and get dressed. When my boyfriend arrived he just walked across the room, he said nothing and hugged me, which was exactly what I needed.

I packed for being away for an unknown length of time. My housemate offered to water my plants and I changed my answerphone message to say I was at my parents. I was in a complete unreality; I even took my suit home thinking I might go to that interview I had in four days time. I did not go: I was too scared to leave the house. I did not believe my sister was really dead and had no conception of the impact of a murder on the survivors.

In the car on the way to my parent's house, I discussed with my younger sister how it could not be Khia who they had found. She had not been identified by anyone who knew her so it couldn't be her. If she had died we hoped she had just slipped and hit her head, or (our least discussed point) if someone hurt her, we hoped she had hurt them too, preferably a lot. My mother told us Khia had been missing for two days, but she had chosen not to tell us. Reuters knew but I did not. We were so close and I did not even know she was missing, and worse than that it was my mother's choice to deny me this information. This did explain to me why my mother told me "Khia is dead", I always wondered why she had not said, "Khia has died", now I understand, to her it was "Khia is missing…Khia is dead". She did not want to worry us but had inadvertently caused us massive amounts of pain. We wanted to be worried; we did not want to continue living normally while her body lay undiscovered, while her murderers escaped and while her companion and the police searched

for her. It has taken me six months to be able to say "Khia's body", instead
of just Khia, when I was talking about her body after she had died.

The next day we heard by telephone from the equivalent of the State
Department that Khia had been murdered. My father was working overseas and was on his way home but was not back yet. My mother was on
the phone, we three sat on the sofa in a row. When they told her, my
mother exclaimed, "murdered!" They asked if we wanted to know how?
Yes we did, they said she was stabbed, "stabbed!" Did we want to know
where? We wanted to know. "In the chest and head", "in the head!" my
mother repeated for us and as an expression of her shock and disbelief.
Did we want to know how many times? Yes, we did, we were told sixteen
times, "sixteen times!" my mother repeated. Apparently we were told Khia
died quickly but I do not remember this. The majority of these details we
were given at first were wrong but they set my mind racing. There is no
evidence to substantiate that she died quickly. We know she was not left to
die and that her murderers made sure they had killed her. But given that
we have a four-hour time span for her time of death, we do not know how
long her ordeal lasted.

For the next two days the media called continually at my parent's and
their neighbor's doors. We tried to notify as many people as we could
before Khia's murder was in the newspapers and on TV. Going through
my sisters address book to call her friends felt so bizarre, so disrespectful.

I have now got more used to the horror of my sister's murder; I hate the
idea of ever getting used to murder. This feels like I am more resigned, and
more depressed. When we first heard I was in such severe shock I could
not leave my parents house. My trust of the world has gone and I now feel
I have to stay alert to stay one step ahead (because I don't know when the
book will end and I want justice). The day I heard about Khia's death, I
opened the wardrobe where all her work suits hung and stroked them and
cried. To me they represented the clothes we bought together, clothes I
helped her choose, clothes I had the same but in another color. It was also
her unfulfilled potential I saw in her work clothes and I could imagine her

standing there in them smiling and asking me what I thought. She had been away too long for her clothes to still retain her smell and it took me weeks to find something which still smelled of her (her pillow).

In the first month I kept searching through her bookcase. Looking for a note to explain, looking for something from her to say, "No, it's not true I am really alive, I'm at this place and this is how you can get to me". It makes so much more sense for her to be alive.

Six weeks later we buried Khia; it was one of the most traumatic experiences of my life. I felt like there was some hope that somehow she could be revived, cloned even, since we still had her body. That hope went when she was buried. I did not want there to be no hope of her being alive. We exhausted ourselves making her funeral as personal as we could. Some people said they felt it was a spiritual experience or the "best" funeral they had been to. I just wanted to jump into her grave with her. I hated to see her coffin so far down in the ground and think of the earth crushing her lovely body when it was piled on top. The digger for the cemetery sat there revving his engine as we left. He just could not wait to fill in her grave. I found it so disturbing to think of her alone in the cemetery that night all alone. I felt like the funeral was for everyone else. Some people felt it helped them "let go" or get a wake-up call about their own lives. I was disgusted. I wanted to world to stop turning; her life was more significant than a wake-up call. I did not want to live another day when I was alive and Khia had been murdered. She was my buffer against growing up in the world; she was the third part of our sibling triangle. I feel like I have lost my balance, I feel so lost without her.

If you can imagine a murder mystery on television, an Agatha Christie novel, or even a game of Cleudo, you know how important all those little details are. How friends may argue about "who dunit". How certain authors are admonished for leaving out vital clues until they reveal all at the end of the book, so you never can guess who the murderer is. You never can be one step ahead because you just don't have all the information. Lots of people have asked why it matters what happened to Khia.

Maybe you can see how important the details are when your loved one is murdered. Not everyone wants all the details, my parents do not but I do, everyone is a little bit different. After I have lost so, so much, I want something back. I want information; I want my questions answered, at the very least. Given the country of Khia's murder, this may seem an impossible task but that is no reason not to try. The way I see it, if we can get things right in Europe for dealing with such an isolated country, we should he able to get it right for dealing with a murder in any other country.

I do not want others to have to go through what we have been through. I could speak for hours about the problems we have had. I am not naming countries because of the political sensitivity. We have been coordinating Khia's murder investigation ourselves and playing detective, ridiculous but true. We have been laughed at in meetings about my sister's case with our State Department equivalent. Intimate evidence is up for public discussion. May be no one told them that it is hard to be objective with strangers in a business-type meeting about your sisters murder. There is no one in our whole State Department equivalent that is trained to deal with murder bereavement. No one even keeps a tally of how many of our country folk are murdered overseas. It took six weeks to get a photofit done in Europe, of a man seen in the area my sister was murdered, with a knife on the day before her murder.

I have no energy for life except my anger that drives me to seek justice and change in the way murders like this are treated. I wish I could work on my sister's case without my incredible anger but I have no other energy left. This has traumatized me too much, for too long. The details we have change over time, they get worse, or get better (better is defined as less suffering for Khia), or the facts get worse again, the details get accurate somewhere along the line we hope. It is an unending process. This casework does serve as a constructive outlet for my anger, which I believe, is healthy.

After seeing a very helpful Victims Advocate a month ago I realized that all my work on Khia's case could not bring her back. There were Christmas decorations up in the City and it really hit me, I just about made it home, driving the wrong way up a one-way street on the way. When I got home I was not capable of conversation; I could not use a knife to prepare my dinner. I went to bed early and was out of it for the next few days.

I am a different person than I was seven months ago. Now I want children and that is about the only thing I know I want because my whole world has been turned upside down. I realize that unless I have a job that is my life's mission, work is just not important. I am very slowly finding a few truths that will hold in my new reality, with which to one day build a new framework to live my life. I am guessing that this can be done. The beliefs which allowed me to walk around and function before are now all irrelevant except one. Therefore walking around and functioning has been very hard. I congratulate myself on the minor miracle of getting up in the morning. The only belief that has helped me is that "Bad things happen to good people". Now this has been replaced with, "horrific things happen to the people I love most in the world". I am now closer to my younger sister. When I see her now I just want to touch her and hold her, she is so precious to me. I just want to feel that she is real and she is still here for me, which she is. We had a day of hanging onto each other through the crowds Christmas Shopping recently. A part of the great thing about the day was to be able to hold her for so long.

Most of those Saturday-night-friends I have never heard from or seen since Khia's murder. People have used any excuses they can to avoid me, even those I considered close friends. I have told others, "tell people to call me, I find it to hard to call out, I want to talk. People don't need to know what to say, just that they are sorry, I need to know they care". I then hear from others why these people have not called me, they feel they need my permission! I was obviously not clear enough. As all my certainties have now gone, I needed the extra reassurance from friends who care, which I did get. One friend 'phoned twice a day for the first few months.

I am needing to build new relationships with my friends who have stayed around and nothing is secure. I need to tell them how to help me best, as I would need someone to tell me if I was in their shoes. I tell them, I don't need you advice on how to grieve, I will ask for advice when I need it, please don't try and fix me. I can not watch murder on TV any more (and to be honest there is not that much left on TV). I can not bear to hear about violence or murder for entertainment. I find it hard hearing about my friends siblings, I know feel this yawning gap, when we exchange sibling news and I say my younger sister is doing this…and there is stops. I could talk about Khia's murder investigation as a consolation but her life and living will always be more important than her murderers or her murder.

I have post-traumatic stress disorder as a result of Khia's murder. This makes perfect sense to me. I have had the worst shock and trauma of my life by a long way. I have had major traumas before but this is on another scale completely and feels more like mental illness to me than anything else I have ever experienced. I must emphasize it is not mental illness, I am having a normal reaction to an abnormal event. My body is doing its job really well in protecting me. It's like my body is saying, "if I see anything that remotely looks like that again, I am going to give you the energy you need to get out of it. I am going to avoid it at all costs. We are not going through that again! Also I am going to keep going over this massive first shock till it makes sense. I need time to do it but I will just keep on at it, and if I see anything in your environment that looks vaguely similar, any extra information I can get I will use it." My consequences are that when I have a conflict about my gas bill on the 'phone, my body prepares physiologically for a life or death situation, in my case my whole body shakes. Anyone could be a murderer; I have narrowed this down to any man, and narrowed it down a bit further to any man wearing clothing that could conceal a knife. In Winter in Europe this is about half of the population and Christmas crowds take on a whole other dimension. I am constantly hyper alert looking for information for something that never will make sense, looking for answers that will never be good enough. I have images of my sister's murder (from autopsy evidence) which play on repeat in my head for hours, hoping that an answer will come up. This makes doing anything including sleeping impossible. Each time we get new information, this whole process starts anew, that is if it has had time to simmer down since the last shock. I have also had visual hallucinations, diarrhea (when we get new traumatic news or have a difficult meeting coming up), difficulty breathing in and after seven months my appetite is sporadic at best.

I have told that the pain never goes away, and it does not get less with time, it just becomes less often. I have been told that "closure" or "getting over it" does not exist except to theorists and those who find it hard to see us in pain. I have been told I will never forget my sister, this really helps! I have been told that grief is harder to bear with time because it is longer since you have seen the person who has died. I have many new friends whose loved ones have been murdered too. It is a club where we need each other so much but nobody wants to be there. I have so much guilt, I have traced back most of the things I could have done to make sure she was a few days behind in her itinerary, or that she never went away at all. But I was never given the choice, do this or your sister will be murdered. She was never given a choice to live either. Khia has lost her whole life and the world has lost a wonderful person. She has lost all her future experiences, her plans and those things that unfold in ways that are better than you ever could imagine. She will never have children, marry or be that excellent Auntie my children deserve. Just living an ordinary life, one person can make sure a difference in the world, especially to those they love. Who knows any of our future contributions?

Sometimes I get glimpses of life in a new normal. I suppose time will tell but at least I am not expecting it to heal me.

~ Anonymous, Europe

EPILOGUE

If I had a dollar for every time someone has told me to "get over it" I would be rich beyond my wildest dreams. What I feel as a nagging need to explain myself to others is violent death is not something that can easily be passed over. We are forever changed when we lose anybody but to lose someone to a violent act is different and nags at our heart on a daily basis.

I hope by sharing this book that perhaps more understanding can come of what it is like to lose a loved one to violence. *Waking To Tears* barely touches the surface of the pain and emotions that are carried with violent loss.

I am not saying that because of losing a loved one to violence we are incapable of living our lives. We do live our lives, we move on, we have to or we lose our own existence. But our attitude changes, we appreciate the life that exists, we perceive the world differently. Our perception has negative and positive outcomes. This is because we are all individuals, we all live, breathe and feel differently. We own our feelings and no one can take that from anyone else.

Several months after my mother's death I was told I changed too much. I knew I changed but at the same time I was only beginning to grieve. I had changed because I didn't make the phone call I wanted to make and then my mother was gone. Now if I have something to say, I will say it whether someone wants to hear me or not. I also live my life for today because we never know what tomorrow holds. Now my changes can be perceived differently by different people but for me this is how I choose to live my life.

For myself, I have gone through the resentment, the anger, weeks of not leaving my home, weeks of fearing the world, hours of wondering what the chances are of losing someone to violence and a sad empty void in my heart that will never completely heal. I have spent years of hiding pain, years of grieving and years of missing a loved one. In many cases, when a loved one dies, especially a violent death, there is a part inside of us that has died with them.

Now that both my parents are gone and I am determined to face this pain, I have learned all the memories that I shoved away. I hid happy memories because I felt they were too painful but have now learned they are a part of who I am and it's okay. I have tried to put the pieces together on why this happens to people. There is always a piece missing to the puzzle, just as there are pieces missing to my heart.

The violent loss of both my parents still shows up in my daily self. I can be insecure, impulsive and scared. My biggest obstacle beyond the grief will be dealing with abandonment issues. I fear losing anyone in my life, I fear becoming close with anyone because I don't want to be abandoned again. My own emotional survival skills can rear their ugly head at any moment of any day and jeopardize more of who I am.

There are no magical words that will take the pain away. There is no magic pill, cure or years of therapy that will make everything all better. I doubt if the hurt ever completely disappears. There are people, real people and ordinary people who share a pain and need others to listen, share and be patient with who we are as a person.

We will have good days and we will have bad days. We have memories that are treasured within us. We will push people away when we need them the most. Be patient, caring, open your mind and heart to see that we have lost more than words can ever describe. We have lost a part of ourselves.

CONCLUSION

We live our lives thinking horrific events won't happen to us. We shouldn't have to live in fear. For too many of us the reality is violence has turned parts of our life into horrific memories and evoked a fear inside us. Everyone must realize that no one is immune to violence.

Violence can touch anyone. Violence doesn't limit itself to race, religion, sex or economic conditions. Violence knows no boundaries.

With this in mind, have compassion for those who carry the weight of how violence has touched their life. Remember not to judge what has happened to someone that you know, you have seen in the media or heard by word of mouth. Anyone can be a victim. When we lose some-one to violence, we too become victims and we lose a part of ourselves.

Victims need understanding, a caring ear and support system. Victims have been changed. Some changes are controllable and some changes are beyond our control. We can't take back the past, we can't change events, we can only hope and pray that fewer people will feel what we feel.

Patience and time is precious. If you can offer patience and time to someone you love, this may be one of the greatest gifts that can be given.

ABOUT THE AUTHOR

Traci Bieber Nelson attended Temple University with a degree in Communications and Mass Media. Her articles have appeared in various newspapers and magazines. She is actively involved in victim services and various volunteer organizations. Ms. Nelson resides in Pennsylvania with her daughters and cats.

NOTES

If you have lost a loved one to violence and would like to share your story for future publication, please contact Traci Bieber Nelson at PO Box 819, Ambler, PA 19002-0819. Ms. Nelson can also be contacted through her website periwinklekid.com. Submissions are open to everyone who has lost a loved one to violence.

Submissions are being accepted by children in two separate age categories of ages 6-12 and 13-19. Parental/Guardian permission is needed for all submissions from children. Information, submission guidelines, and release forms are available by contacting Ms. Nelson at the above-mentioned address.

A percentage of quarterly sales of this book will be donated to various victim service organizations. The victim service organizations are those recommended by the book's contributors.